IMAGES
of England

ILKLEY

Ilkley, *c.* 1835.

IMAGES
of England

ILKLEY

*To Pat and Dick
with best wishes
Mike Dixon*

Compiled by
Mike Dixon

TEMPUS

Tempus Publishing Limited
The Mill, Brimscombe Port,
Stroud, Gloucestershire, GL5 2QG

ISBN 0 7524 1507 7

Typesetting and origination by
Tempus Publishing Limited
Printed in Great Britain by
Midway Clark Printing, Wiltshire

View of Ilkley from Middleton, *c.* 1900.

Contents

Acknowledgements

This book could not have been compiled without the help of numerous people. While the majority of photographs are from my personal collection, they have been supplemented from several other sources. I am particularly indebted to Sally Brown who has allowed me generous access to her extensive collection of old Ilkley postcards. I would also like to thank Eric Daniels of the University of Leeds Media Services, for access to the Godfrey Bingley Collection; the staff of Ilkley Public Library; Gavin Edwards of the Manor House Museum; and several private collectors, notably David Harrison, Tim Mutton, Jack and Joyce Tipping and Peter West.

I am grateful to many other individuals who have given me valuable information and/or photographs, including Jack Bentley, Paul Bourgeois, Shirley Bowness, Jennifer Cawood, Alan Cawthra, John Chambers, Dorothy Cockroft, John Cockshott, Scilla Douglas, John Fisher, Jane Forster, Jim Horsley, Kath Hunter, Heather Hutchins, Heather Hutchinson, Frazer Irwin, Ann Kilvington, Margery McDonald, Sandra Monger, May Pickles, Roger Pyrah, Gwen Robinson, Dorothy Smithson, Ronnie Stowell, Gordon Sugden, Andrew Walbank, Roy Walker and Barry Wilkinson. In collecting images over the past twenty-five years there will be some sources that I have failed to acknowledge. If you are among the names I should have mentioned, please accept my apoligies.

I acknowledge the assistance gained from previous local history publications featuring archive photographs including *Ilkley Remembered* (Olicana Museum and Historical Society, 1976), *Images of Ilkley* (Local Studies Department, City of Bradford Metropolitan Council, 1982), *Ilkley in old picture postcards* (Keith Davies, European Library, Netherlands, 1985) and *Ilkley, the Victorian era* by David Carpenter (Smith Settle, 1986). I am also indebted to a series of historical articles published in the *Ilkley Gazette* in the 1970s contributed by the then editor, Mr R.M. Green. Likewise the *Gazette* column 'Across the Years', compiled by former editor Brian Lynch, has been a valuable source of information.

I would like to thank Steve Toms and David J. Stansfeld Bailey for their expert photographic assistance. They have converted lantern slides, book plates, fading sepia and precious postcards into prints suitable for publication.

Finally I would like to express my thanks and gratitude to my wife Judy for introducing me to the delights of Ilkley and for constantly supporting my somewhat obsessive interest in old photographs and the stories behind them.

Introduction

Ilkley is self-evidently a Victorian town but its extraordinary growth between 1837 and 1901 perhaps deserves further emphasis. In the 1820s Ilkley was described as 'one of the most rustic, inaccessible and primitive little places in the country. The streets are full of ruts and holes and lined by stinking refuse'. In addition to ruts and holes Brook Street also had a brook running down the middle! Yet by the end of the century it was established as a substantial inland resort and a desirable place to live for the business and professional classes of Bradford and Leeds. These impressions are borne out by the census returns; in 1841 the population of Ilkley township was 778 while in 1901 this had grown to 7,455. This roughly ten-fold increase is far in excess of 'natural' growth and signifies substantial migration to the town.

Despite its small and impoverished state at the beginning of the Victorian era, Ilkley has very old foundations. The carved rocks on the Moor bear testimony to some kind of settlement in the Early Bronze Age around 1800 BC and are found close to the line of Rombalds Way, a prehistoric trade route. The town's Roman associations are well known and 'Olicana' was the site of a succession of military forts from the first wooden structure erected by Agricola in AD 80 to a stone fort which survived until the end of the Roman occupation in the late fourth or early fifth century. The Romans left behind a small and undistinguished civilian settlement that became just another Anglo-Saxon village in Wharfedale.

In the medieval period the village appears to have had two open-fields, the west field centred along an access lane along the line of Kings Road and the east field along the line of Little Lane. A pattern of enclosed fields then emerged, but with little growth in the size of the village. Most of the land was owned by the Lord of the Manor who, from 1484 until 1904 was a member of the Middleton family.

The village had little that distinguished it from its neighbours until around 1690 when a bathhouse was built close to the origin of a moorland spring – White Wells. At first the bathhouse catered largely for the locals as there were 'no public conveyances in or out of the place' until the 1830s. Despite this, by 1841 Granville in his book on Northern Spas was writing of Ilkley, 'It is not the fashion to dwell more than a fortnight or a month in this region; although it is perfectly, strictly and imperatively fashionable for people in the North to come to Ilkley, or at all events, to say that they have been at Ilkley.'

Thereafter three events shaped the rapid development of the town. In 1843 a merchant and Lord Mayor of Leeds, Hamer Stansfeld JP, introduced the recently described technique of hydrotherapy (the Water Cure) to Ilkley and this culminated in the building of Britain's first hydropathic hotel, the Ben Rhydding Hydro. The second development was the arrival of the railway in 1865. The railway provided good connections with Leeds and Bradford and, after

1888, the extension to Skipton provided access from the industrial towns of Lancashire. The middle classes saw a visit to Ilkley as the thing to do, and would use their stay in the 'Malvern of the North' to explore the idylls of Wharfedale. The working man could take advantage of the many cheap rail excursions that ran from the northern industrial towns and bring his family to this mecca of factory society. The third factor in Ilkley's growth was the release of Manorial land for public and private building by the Middletons. The first sale in 1867 provided an opportunity for considerable building development around the centre of the town and many notable buildings were erected in the following three or four years. Subsequent land sales up to the close of the century allowed domestic building around Parish Ghyll Road, Queens Road, Grove Road and Easby Drive giving the town its essentially Victorian character.

This compilation of photographs seeks to document these events and the changes that they brought about in Ilkley. From a starting point of the legacy of pre-Victorian buildings, the book traces the arrival of hydrotherapy and the town's development as an inland resort – The Heather Spa. The consequent changes in the town are then reflected in a detailed examination of the three principal streets, Brook Street, Church Street and The Grove. Other aspects of the town's growth, its public and private institutions, its schools and churches are explored while the pictorial record is enlivened by people, parades, and processions marking the passing of local and national events. The pictorial record has of course been the subject of previous publications but I have tried to avoid too much repetition of published images except when the item is of particular interest or relevance to the narrative. I hope that even the local history enthusiasts will find much that is new in this collection.

As an 'off-comed-un', albeit with over thirty years acquaintance with Ilkley, there is much local history that I do not know. Although I have endeavoured to check my sources, there will no doubt be inadvertent errors in the details presented here. I hope that readers will alert me to any mistakes or shortcomings, so that they may be corrected in a second edition should one follow this one.

Mike Dixon
March 1999

One
The Pre-Victorian
Legacy

Thatched cottages in Skipton Road, c. 1865. The occupants of these cottages have lined up outside while the wagoner stands erect to ensure his place at centre stage. The buildings reveal the poverty of much of the pre-Victorian legacy; the village consisting largely of such single-storey cottages thatched with heather from the Moor. These stood opposite the Listers Arms Hotel (built as the New Inn for John Lister in 1825). Box Tree Cottage (farmhouse) is on the right, hidden by the trees.

Castle House, Bridge Lane, *c.* 1900. This handsome house represents the other end of the range of pre-Victorian housing. The house is eighteenth century with a particularly fine doorcase in the style of Gibbs whose designs flourished from 1720 onwards. It was subsequently split into two with the construction of a second doorway to the right of the original. At the time portrayed the house was used as refreshment rooms and apartments by Mrs Horner. The name 'Castle House' is an association with the so-called 'Castle' – now the Manor House museum.

The Old Bridge, *c.* 1900. In the Roman period the Wharfe was crossed by a simple ford and this must have sufficed for the next millenium. The existence of a bridge is recorded in the early seventeenth century but this was washed away and rebuilt in 1638. However, in the great Wharfedale flood of 1673 the Ilkley Bridge was swept away as were the bridges at Bolton Abbey, Barden, Burnsall and Kettlewell. The present bridge dates from 1675 but repairs were required on several occasions before the end of the century. Over the ensuing 300 years the bridge has been battered by numerous floods but has withstood them all and survives, albeit closed to traffic, as a picturesque feature of our town.

The 'Old Castle' (Manor House), 1867. One of a series of postcards issued by John Shuttleworth utilising photographs from the 1860s and providing an invaluable record of mid-Victorian Ilkley. Both 'Castle' and 'Manor House' are misnomers. The building was originally a yeoman farmer's house of the fourteenth century but dates mostly from the seventeenth century. The name 'Castle' was used in the early Victorian era and no doubt derives from 'castrum' – the Roman fort. This is reasonable because much of the masonry derived from the walls of the fort. The cottages in Castle Yard (those on the right were demolished in 1969) were largely occupied by woolcombing families and handloom weavers according to the 1841 census. It was opened as the Manor House museum in July 1961 by Percy Dalton a local benefactor.

The Rose and Crown, 1869. Ilkley's oldest hostelry, the Rose and Crown, was one of the badges of the House of Lancaster and was adopted by John of Gaunt, 'Lord of the Honor and Forest of Knaresbro' whose kinsman Sir Robert de Plesyngton became Lord of the Manor of Ilkley in 1400. There was already an inn, probably on this site, recorded in the Poll Tax returns of 1378. In 1869 the landlord was William Kendall. The sign reads 'Carriages and Post Horses for Hire' reminding us that this was the principal coaching inn in the village.

Robert Collyer's old smithy, 1868. The smithy stood on Leeds Road opposite the extension to The Crescent Hotel. Robert Collyer was a Victorian hero who rose from humble beginnings as the village blacksmith to become one of the great pulpit figures of America. The smithy boasts a dovecote (and a 'pigeon ladder' against the wall) as well as a grindstone and a public notice board! One of Ilkley's many donkeys is being shoed. The smithy was demolished in 1878 to make way for shops.

Robert Collyer, aged 76. Collyer came to Ilkley from his home in Blubberhouses at the age of 14 (in 1838) to serve an apprenticeship with the blacksmith John (Jackie) Birch. He finished his apprenticeship in 1844 at the age of 21 and was then paid 18 shillings per week. Collyer worked at the Leeds Road smithy until 1850 when, after a series of personal tragedies, he emigrated with his new (second) wife, Ann Longbottom, to America. After emigration Collyer secured employment in a claw hammer factory in Philadelphia. He had left Ilkley as a local Methodist preacher and during his early years in America he pursued this calling. However he became increasingly disenchanted with the Methodist Church and in 1859 he gave up factory work and took a position as an 'outreach' minister with the Unitarian Church in Chicago. He subsequently founded a hugely popular Second Unitarian Church and his reputation as a preacher continued to grow. In 1879 he accepted an invitation to become Pastor of the main Unitarian Church in New York. He continued to preach until a few weeks before his death in 1912.

Old houses in Leeds Road 1867. These substantial houses stood at the junction of Weston Road and Leeds Road. The cottage at the right has been added at a later date as can be seen from the difference in the roof slates and the size of the windows. Note the change from the horizontally sliding 'Yorkshire Sash' window at the top left to the later vertical sash type on the right which allows two of the children of the household to gaze out. The woman with a baby sitting on the branch of a tree is Mrs Stephenson whose husband, Tom, was a wheelwright.

The top of Brook Street, from an engraving by Revd Thomas Kilby, c. 1835. This is one of a series of four etchings sold in aid of the Ilkley Bath Charity and is a much copied picture of 'Old Ilkley'. The thatch in the centre is now the site of Dacre, Son and Hartley, but the house with the smoking chimney (to the left) still stands in Wells Road.

Down Brook Street, *c.* 1800. Based on an old engraving, this view shows the low parapet bridge that crossed the town brook at the top of the street and a second bridge of the simple 'clapper' type about mid-way down. Although picturesque, we have to remember that in the absence of a sewerage system, the brook acted as a drain for 'liquid refuse' and according to Collyer 'the street was lined by a choice collection of stinking middens'.

Hawksworth's Farm, 1867. The dilapidated house and outbuildings of William Hawsworth's farm ran at right angles to Brook Street. They were demolished in 1868 to provide a building plot for Shuttleworth's new emporium, Gothic House (see p. 40).

Cottages and shops in Brook Street, 1866. These buildings on the west side of Brook Street are of considerable antiquity. The thatch in the centre is of ancient 'cruck' frame construction and an extension had to be added to create Joseph Ickringill's grocery shop. The shop next door belonged to Joseph Ramsden, a general draper, while the thatch at the left belonged to Walter Shoesmith, boot and shoe maker.

Old cottages opposite the railway station, 1867. These cottages were situated in what is now Station Road and were in a dilapidated condition at the time portrayed. Even when newly constructed they would have been very meagre dwellings with only one or two rooms and floors of stone-flags or compacted earth. They would have looked more attractive in the summer when the heather thatch sprouted saxifrage and house leeks but this would not disguise their primitive nature. The cottages were demolished in 1868 to make way for the Midland Hotel and shops.

Hartley's farmhouse 1867. The postcard is labelled 'The Manor House', which is another misnomer although the term was applied to this building in the Victorian era. It was situated on an elevated plateau of land on the then Green Lane (The Grove) between what is now Wells Walk and Riddings Road. Although originally a farm, the Hartley family were largely occupied in wool combing in the 1841 census. It was demolished in 1868 to make way for shops and offices.

Green Lane Cottage 1867. This was the only other building in Green Lane and was occupied at this time by Miss Vickers. However it had earlier been occupied by Thomas Atkinson, a farmer and lodginghouse keeper. Among his more illustrious lodgers could have been Madame Tussaud, as Harry Speight, writing towards the end of the nineteenth century, claimed that the cottage was 'a favourite resort' of the waxwork impresario. The property was demolished in 1891 to make way for shops and houses and the site is now occupied by Betty's Café.

Low Hall, *c.* 1890. This property situated off Rupert Road is arguably Ilkley's oldest intact house and contains fragments of medieval stonework. It was built by the Middletons – hence the full name Myddelton Low Hall, the 'Low' serving to distinguish it from their later residence higher up the hillside, Myddelton Lodge. The Middletons were devout Roman Catholics and the room over the porch, partly obscured by the huge walnut tree, was used as a chapel for covert services. The house also had a fine fish pond and was famous for its tench. The property was occupied by the Alderson family for much of the Victorian period.

Wheatley Hall, *c.* 1880. A handsome seventeenth-century building forming the main feature of the then hamlet of Wheatley and now found adjacent to the station at Ben Rhydding. It was probably built by the Bolling family and had links with that family until 1852 when it passed to the Mawson family. However the 1851 census also reveals Richard Ellis (a kinsman of the Ellis's at Hollin Hall) and Henry Kettlewell, their wives and their children in residence. The Mawsons encouraged the Methodist cause by holding services in the kitchen of the Hall.

Myddelton Lodge, *c*. 1880. This sixteenth-century house was the home of the Lords of the Manor of Ilkley, the Middletons, for several centuries. It was reputedly a hunting lodge built by the Percy family who had been granted the manor of Ilkley after the Norman Conquest. The Middleton family moved there from Low Hall around 1600 after marrying into the Percy line. The family held the Manor directly until 1763 when William Middleton died with no heir. The Manor passed to his sister's grandson, William Constable, who then changed his name to Middleton! His son Peter died in 1866 and it was probably because of his extravagance that his heir, Charles Marmaduke Middleton had to sell off parts of his estate. Charles sold the manorial rights in 1893 and the Lodge itself in 1898 and left Ilkley shortly afterwards. He died in Ripon in 1904. His death marked the end of a 400 year family association with the manor of Ilkley. The Lodge was tenanted for a while and eventually sold to Mr Sidney Kellet, a Bradford merchant and JP, who was living at the Briery in Kings Road. The Kellet family modernised the Lodge without altering its basic Elizabethan character and, although they were Anglicans who worshipped at St Margaret's, they scrupulously preserved the Roman Catholic chapel. However the altar, the Stations of the Cross and communion rails had already been transferred to the Church of the Sacred Heart in Stockeld Road. Mr Kellet died in 1920 and the Lodge and estate were acquired by the Passionist Fathers in 1922. The religious nature of the house was reflected in its new name – St Paul's Retreat. Extra accommodation for the Retreat House was added in the 1930s. The Passionist Fathers left the Lodge in 1985 and the house was taken over by the Roman Catholic Diocese of Leeds as a Pastoral and Ecumenical centre.

Two
Water, Water Everywhere

White Wells, 1890. The old White Wells building on the moorside seems to encapsulate the spirit of Ilkley, and this is entirely appropriate. Not only does it represent a picturesque landmark, it marks the site of the first bathhouse and the foundation of Ilkley as a spa town. The bathhouse was built around 1690, close to the spring which supplied the town brook. The buildings were restored and enlarged in 1780 thanks to the munificence of William Middleton. The separate block on the right was erected in 1829 and housed the Charity Bath. It now houses the toilets!

The drinking fountain, White Wells, c. 1880. The custodian of White Wells, William Butterfield, holds the chained pewter tankard that enabled the visitor to take a cool draught of the moorland water. The original postcard bears the caption 'An undiluted beverage from the heart of Rombald's Moor, Ilkley'. This beverage was frequently analysed but found to contain no dissolved minerals, so it was promoted because of its softness and purity which 'makes it more efficacious by passing sooner to the utmost and finest limits of the circulation than any water known'!

The plunge bath, White Wells, c. 1880. This Roman style plunge bath held 1,150 gallons of almost ice-cold water (40°F) into which the intrepid bather would descend in order to experience the manifold benefits of cold water immersion. A second bath is now dry and lies under the floor in the west wing, here a shower bath, of equally cold water could be taken. It was the presence of this bathhouse and the reputation of Ilkley as an inland spa which led the entrepreneurial Hamer Stansfeld JP of Headingley to establish 'The Water Cure' in the village.

West View and the Mill Dam, *c.* 1870. The lowest building on the left contained Edward Usher's boarding house and it was here in March 1843 that Hamer Stansfeld installed Dr Antoine Rischanek to conduct a hydrotherapy practice using the baths at White Wells. This followed Stansfeld's own successful introduction to The Water Cure under the care of its founder – Vincent Priessnitz in Grafenberg, Silesia. The Water Cure necessitated frequent applications of ice-cold water by baths, showers, douches and the like, a regime which Ilkley was well able to deliver. The mill dam was drained soon after this and two houses, Linndale and Millbrook, were erected on the site.

Ben Rhydding from the east, *c.* 1865. Such was the success of Dr Rischanek's practice in West View that Stansfeld decided to erect a purpose-built hotel for hydrotherapy. He purchased 65 acres of land above Wheatley from Mr Bolling in the summer of 1843, and building of the hydro, to be called Ben Rhydding, began immediately. The hotel opened on 29 May 1844 and, despite the rival claims of Malvern, was the first hydro to be built in England. It cost approximately £30,000. However, it proved not to be the financial success Stansfeld anticipated until Rischanek was dismissed and Dr William McLeod was appointed physician in 1847.

View of Ben Rhydding Hydro from the Cow and Calf Rocks, *c*. 1870. The hotel is seen in its heyday. Thanks to McLeod's good stewardship (he purchased the hydro in 1863) the building virtually doubled in size and could accommodate 160 visitors. It also boasted Turkish Baths – erected in 1859 at a cost exceeding £2,000 – and the unique compressed-air bath, a McLeod invention which was later reproduced at other hydropathic centres. By then the grounds occupied about 200 acres. Many of the visitors took excursions including hiring a carriage to view the dramatic rocks at close quarters. McLeod left Ben Rhydding in 1873 and died two years later.

Wells House Hydro, *c*. 1900. This was the second hydro to appear in Ilkley. A company was formed in 1853 and land purchased from Peter Middleton. The building, erected at a cost of £30,000, opened in May 1856. It was designed by the most successful architect in Yorkshire, Cuthbert Broderick, and the extensive grounds were laid out by the landscape gardener, Mr Major. The first physician at Wells House was Dr Rischanek but he fared no better here than at Ben Rhydding for he only lasted two years and was replaced by Dr Edmund Smith. The hydro changed hands several times over the next eighty years, but latterly one constant feature was the presence of Mr Robins.

William Henry Robins, *c.* 1939. Mr Robins was brought up in Oxford and came to Wells House as a young man to work as a 'boots', a general servant. He became head porter and was a familiar figure in his splendid dark green and gold uniform greeting guests as they arrived at the main door. He worked at Wells House for over fifty years and lived with his family in Wells House Lodge, one of two stone cottages that still stand close to the lower entrance. The other cottage, Ivy Lodge, was occupied for many years by Mr and Mrs William Hutchinson. In 1917 Mr Hutchinson had charge of the livery stables behind the cottages but ten years later the stables had become Wells House Garage and Mr Hutchinson had become a motor engineer. After the war Wells House was purchased on behalf of the Society of Jesuits, but they never took possession; then by the Ministry of Labour and National Service for use as a hostel for European Volunteer Workers; and finally became a Domestic Science College (later the Bradford and Ilkley Community College) admitting its first students in 1952.

Wells Terrace, *c.* 1890. Among the early visitors to Wells House perhaps the most noteworthy was Charles Darwin. Darwin arrived on 3 October 1859 and after two weeks of treatment under Dr Smith was joined by his family. At this point he rented an apartment from Marshall Hainsworth in Wells Terrace (now Hillside) and continued to consult Dr Smith. However his opinion of Smith was less than flattering. Darwin wrote 'Dr Smith...they all say...is very careful in bad illness but he constantly gives me the impression as if he cared very much for the fee and very little for the patient.' On 24 November 1859 his *Origin of Species* was published and Darwin immediately suffered a severe relapse!

Craiglands Hydropathic Establishment, *c.* 1900. Built in 1859 by Michael Dobson, Craiglands has been a relatively successful enterprise and is the only hydro to survive as a hotel to the present day. The original building seen to the right accommodated forty 'patients' but two further extensions brought the capacity in 1900 up to 200 guests. Jabez and Henry Dobson took over from their father, with Henry becoming the resident physician. His credentials were well suited to practice in Ilkley. After qualifying in Edinburgh, he was for six months resident doctor at the Brompton Hospital for Consumption and Diseases of the Chest. He also boasted of being 'Late Physician with Viscount Strangford in Bulgaria', although why he was 'late' is not explained.

Craiglands' ballroom, *c.* 1900. The ballroom featured strongly in Craiglands' publicity material. At 85 feet long, 37 feet wide and 26 feet high it was 'the largest and best recreation hall in England' and ideal for the evening amusements 'which are the best at any Hydro in the country'. For the Autumn Ball (19 October 1900) 'the whole of this immense area, except the row of seats around, is available for the gyratory motions of the terpsichorean art'. What the occupants of the bedrooms around the ballroom thought of the band is not recorded.

Troutbeck Hydro, *c.* 1900. Troutbeck (in Crossbeck Road) was erected in 1863 by Dr Edmund Smith as a more modest alternative to Wells House. However his reign was short lived for by 1867 the hotel was owned by Dr William P. Harrison (also physician at Wells House) and managed by Miss Wilkinson. The terms were £2 16s per week but there were substantial reductions for visits between October and May. The Troutbeck survived until recently as a hotel, indeed Prince Charles stayed here on two occasions in the 1970s when he visited Yorkshire for the grouse-shooting on the Duke of Devonshire's estate.

The Spa Hydro, *c.* 1900. Originally built as 'The Grove' Hydropathic Establishment in 1864, it was renamed 'The Spa', around 1885 when it came under the management of Mrs Lee. Dr Thomas Johnstone was the visiting physician. In order to compete with its more established rivals, their advertisements declared 'The Sanatorium is situated in The Grove, and being at a less elevation than others of the kind, it finds favour with that class of people whose enfeebled condition renders them unable to take that energetic exertion required in climbing to such commanding altitudes.'

The Stoney Lea Hydro, *c.* 1900. This hydro, seen from the croquet lawn on the eastern aspect, was situated in Cowpasture Road at the junction with Ben Rhydding Road. It was built in 1880 by Tom Emmott, a former bath-man at Ben Rhydding Hydro. It remained in the Emmott family until 1945 by which time it had become a fully licensed hotel with thirty bedrooms. Thereafter it had a chequered career and was finally demolished in 1981 to be replaced by a cluster of town houses. The houses on the left, Tarn Villas, were built in 1874.

Rockwood House Hydro, *c.* 1890. Opened in 1871 and located just above Tarn Villas and Heatherlands in Cowpasture Road, 'the situation of Rockwood House is unsurpassed, adjoining the heights of Rombalds Moor, and commanding fine views of the scenery for which Wharfedale is so famous.' The proprietor and manager was James Lister and the Consulting Physician was initially Dr Johnstone then Dr Scott. In 1890 the hydro boasted a liberal table – four meals a day – and the terms were 27 shillings per week, all in.

Marlborough House Hydro, *c.* 1900. When it was built in 1878, Marlborough House stood 'at the extreme east of Ilkley, in Clifton Road'. It was built by Jeremiah Barker but it was his wife Sarah, 'a lady who had been associated with hydropathy since its introduction' who was registered as the proprietress. She was evidently desirous of having a larger establishment in so far as she had the photographer draw in an extension to the rear! The hotel was demolished in the early 1970s and replaced by town houses – Marlborough Square.

A tennis party at Marlborough House, *c.* 1885. Among the diversions available at Marlborough House, lawn tennis was obviously popular. The visitors appear to be playing for a handsome trophy (or it could be a tea urn for refreshment between matches). Mrs Barker provided a feast of other entertainments for her visitors which included 'Billiards, Croquet, Bowls, Bagatelle, Chess, Draughts, &c; while the evenings are rendered agreeable by Charades, Games, Dances, Courts of Trial, Readings, Recitations, Musical and other Entertainments of various kinds.' Then, as if to reassure those who view such conviviality with some trepidation, she adds 'Notice – Persons who are of unsound mind, and contagious or objectionable cases, are not admitted to Marlborough House.'

Demolition of Ben Rhydding 1955. The hydros found it increasingly difficult to attract visitors as the twentieth century progressed. Their regimes departed to a greater or lesser degree from hydropathy. The emphasis switched from a hydro resort for the sick to a holiday resort for the healthy – The Heather Spa. Ben Rhydding laid out a nine-hole golf course in its grounds in 1885 and promoted itself as a golf hotel, but with little success. Like Wells House it was requisitioned by the War Office between 1939 and '45 but afterwards remained empty, leading to its demolition in 1954/55. The golf course and two outbuildings, the stables and lodge, survive, as does the name – 'Hydro Close', a small cul-de-sac on the site.

Inscription on the bath in the Canker Well Gardens, 1975. The marble bath is another relic of Ben Rhydding removed from 'The Shrine' in the grounds. Its fading inscription reads 'In honour of Vincent Priessnitz, the Silesian peasant to whom the world is indebted for the blessing of the system of cure by cold water, this fountain is gratefully erected and inscribed by Hamer Stansfeld. Ben Rhydding, XXIX May MDCCCXLIV' (29 May 1844).

Three
The Heather Spa

Although hydropathy only enjoyed a short-lived vogue as a medical treatment, the hydros softened their regimes so that they became attractive to a wider clientele whose main concerns were rest, relaxation and entertainment rather than the rigours of the cold water cure. Hotels and boarding houses were built to accommodate visitors rather than patients and facilities were created to attract the day visitor and tourist to Ilkley. To this end a small group of local worthies proposed that the pond known as Craig Dam be converted into a 'Tarn' with a promenade around it to add to the attractiveness of the Moor. After gaining the approval of Lord of the Manor, William Middleton, and having collected £141 3s 3d by subscription, work commenced in September 1873. The collapse of a dam and disputes with the owners of Craiglands led to delays but the work was finally completed in 1875. There was a fountain on the nearest island fed by gravity from a small reservoir up the hillside.

The Tarn and Pierrots, *c.* 1900. The 600 yard promenade around the Tarn proved to be a popular spot. 'From early in the morning until the afternoon there are always nurses to be found with their young charges, young people with their sketching blocks, or some feminine group whiling away the hours with some antimacassar [embroidery] work. The arrival of twilight is wistfully hailed by another class of visitor when soft whisperings and cupid's marketing begins.' The appeal of the Tarn was no doubt enhanced by the Pierrots.

Cooper's Tarn Pierrots, *c.* 1904. The Pierrots performed three times a day during the holiday season and promoted themselves as 'Ilkley's only amusement: The place to spend a pleasant hour'. The proprietor, Mr C. Cooper, was landlord of the North View (later Station) Hotel and he had gathered together a diverse group of aspiring or fading theatricals. The group was made up of Miss Nora Beverley (soprano vocalist and comedienne), Mr Alec Richards (well-known Scottish bass), Miss Nora Bell (young contralto), Mr J. Bedford Ogden (renowned Yorkshire humorist), Mr Arthur Hanson (celebrated baritone vocalist), Mr Will Ambro (coon vocalist, comedian and dancer) and Miss Nanna Baxter (pianist and mezzo soprano).

Bandstand, West View Park, *c.* 1905. The manorial rights over Ilkley Moor were purchased by the Local Board from Charles Marmaduke Middleton in 1893 for £13,500 thereby providing the people of Ilkley with open access and the Board with all water and sporting rights. As part of the drive towards establishing Ilkley as an attractive inland resort, a small park was created on the fringe of the Moor at the top of Wells Road. Paths were laid out, rustic bridges were built and a handsome bandstand was erected in July 1904 at a cost of £120.

Ilkley and District Council Military Band, 1904. This fine body of musicians, resplendent in their top hats (the programme seller is distinguished by the boater), could be heard regularly during the summer months at the West View Bandstand. The gentleman holding the baton is Mr Wardle S. Bellerby, the Musical Director, who lived in Tivoli Place. In 1899 the band had the good fortune to purchase all the instruments from the trustees of the Calverley Brass Band for £42. The bandstand was demolished during the inter-war years.

White Wells Café, *c.* 1920. A further attraction of a ramble on the Moor came with the building of a café close to White Wells. The tea rooms were run for many years by Mrs Williamson who lived in Chantry Drive, but sadly the property became a target for vandals during the winter months and the Urban District Council decided to remove it in the late 1960s. A similar fate nearly befell White Wells itself, but thanks to the generosity of Eric Busby, the building was restored between 1972 and '74, and refreshments are now available there.

Entrance to Wells Promenade, early 1900s. A delightful snow scene at the foot of Mill Ghyll. At this time the fountain was enclosed by iron railings. The seat in the bottom right corner is one of several around the fountain which in the summer months were a favourite spot for sitting and watching the world go by. Perhaps because of all the chattering that went on it was known as 'The Monkey Rack'.

The fountain, 23 April 1908. A late frost had decorated the fountain with icicles. It was erected in 1875 at a cost of £130, raised by public subscription. Water issued from the nostrils of the four horses and from twenty-one jets around the bottom of the basin. The upper tiers comprised mermaids and serpents. It was demolished in 1959 after repeated attacks of vandalism.

Mill Ghyll, 1909. The dam at the top of Mill Ghyll originally supplied two corn-mills, one being in existence in the thirteenth century. The upper mill was just below Queens Road and the lower situated on the east bank, across what is now Wells Promenade. The land for Mill Ghyll was leased to the Local Board by William Middleton (at a rent of one shilling per annum) in June 1873 and later that year the paths were laid out, a miniature waterfall was constructed, ferns were planted and the fencing was renewed.

The Chalybeate Spring, Heber's Ghyll, *c.* 1890. Public access to this attractive wooded ravine in Briery Wood was granted in 1887 by Charles Marmaduke Middleton. The Ghyll (gill) takes its name from the Heber family of Hollin Hall but was originally known as Black Beck, 'black' being a modern contraction of the Irish 'bealach' – a boundary. The gill is fed by a spring, 'Silver Well', which is likely to have been an old Celtic tutelary spring, that is one into which silver may have been thrown to appease the spirit of the well.

The Crescent Hotel, *c.* 1905. Hotels soon followed in the wake of the hydros. The first to appear was the Crescent, which was built around 1860 at a cost of £8,000. The first manager had the intriguing name of John Baptiste Fleischmann. It boasted ample stabling and coach-house accommodation at the rear, which has recently been converted into small shop units. It also had its own bowling green. The site was originally occupied by a shop belonging to William Bell, and the upper room became known as 't'Ranter's Chamber' because a noisy group of Methodists filled it with much singing and foot stamping.

Middleton Hotel, *c.* 1900. Originally given the short-lived name 'The Victoria', the Middleton was built in 1865-67. During the Second World War it was used as an Officer's Training School under the command of Col. Sebag-Montefiore. It underwent another change of name in 1947 when it became The Ilkley Moor Hotel and was a popular venue for visiting football and rugby league teams playing in the area. The main frontage was in Skipton Road but this view shows both the hotel and the adjoining public bar. The bar survived the fire that destroyed the main hotel on 30 July 1968 and resulted in four deaths. It remains as the Ilkley Moor Vaults ('The Taps').

The Royal Hotel, *c.* 1955. The Royal Hotel was built in the early 1870s on the site of a well known thatch, Mother Downes' Cottage. The hotel was built for Hezekiah Dobson of Holly Bank House, Leeds Road, who continued as proprietor into the 1880s. The hotel was enlarged in 1892. It was demolished in 1962 to be replaced by Wells Court. The Victorian housing lower down Wells Road made way for Wells Mews.

Tarn House, 1892. This property was one of dozens in the town used, at one time or another, as a boarding house. It was situated on the corner of Wheatley Road and Cowpasture Road and was probably built as a private residence. However, by 1881 it had become a ladies' school run by Mrs Annie Wainwright, and in 1892 was a day and boarding school run by the Misses Lawrence. Thereafter it became a boarding house. The foundations of the new grammar school are visible just behind the house, and to the left the houses of Mount Pleasant are clearly seen. In the distance, to the right, is Ilkley Brewery and behind it the main gasometer of Ilkley Gasworks. The house was demolished in 1964.

Boating on the Wharfe, c. 1905. These rowing boats were available for hire from Septimus Wray who had 'Pleasure Gardens' and a boathouse by the riverside. In order to maintain the water level during the summer, small boys would be given a penny to wade out into the river and build up a dam. After the Second World War the boats were owned by Mr Dell for many years.

Opening of the Ilkley Moor Golf Clubhouse, 13 April 1907. Ilkley's first golf course was opened by the Ilkley Golf Club in 1890 on the edge of Rombald's Moor just off the Keighley Gate Road. In 1894, however, the Local Board would not extend the club's lease without a substantial increase in rent, so the club found a new site and by 1898 a new eighteen-hole course had been laid out by the river. The clubhouse was moved down from the Moor, and the old course handed over to a group of tradesmen and workmen who formed the Olicana Golf Club. In 1905 they changed their name to the Ilkley Moor Golf Club and the members are seen here celebrating the opening of their new clubhouse, built between the grounds of the Semon Home and what is now known as Cherry Bank (formerley Rossendale). The two gentlemen holding clubs are James Braidy and Harry Vardon who played an exhibition match. The Moor course was in use until the late 40s.

Ilkley Golf Club clubhouse, c. 1905. The original clubhouse on the Moor course was a four-roomed corrugated iron structure with a veranda. It was erected in 1892 at a cost of £375. When the clubhouse was taken down and re-assembled in its present location it was doubled in size. A spring on the site was utilised for a water supply and an acetylene gas-plant was purchased for heating and lighting. Electricity was not installed until 1928.

The O.H.I.O. Court Minstrels, 1905. 'Blacking-up' to perform songs associated with the American cotton slaves – negro spirituals and the like, was a popular form of entertainment and certainly not seen to be in any way offensive. This group of minstrels performed at a Grand Oriental Bazaar held in Ilkley during Easter Week, 1905. They appear to have been established for at least three years for the postcard bears the legend '…minstrels…who performed before the King' and then in very small print 'was crowned' i.e. in 1902.

The Open Air Bathing Pool, c. 1936. The bathing pool opened in 1934 and immediately became a popular facility. In its first year there were 110,000 bathers and spectators and the receipts were £2,400. Although the Ilkley weather may have been on the cool side, at least the water was heated to a more inviting temperature by a large gas-fired boiler.

Four

Brook Street

Brook Street in 1862. The brook was culverted in 1853 producing an unusually wide carriageway for a Victorian street. On the right a man and woman stand outside Brook Terrace. On the left are houses which, over the course of the following ten years, were all converted into shops. At this stage J.W. Usher's grocery and druggist shop stands in splendid isolation. This shop later became Worfolk's the chemist and much more recently Dickinson's newsagents. The shop at the top facing down Brook Street belonged to John Batty, grocer, druggist and porter merchant.

Brook Terrace, 1863. This terrace, built in 1855, was the first purpose-built shop premises with housing above to be erected in Ilkley. To the left is Hawksworth's farmhouse which was demolished to make way for a larger shop for John Shuttleworth whose 'fancy goods repository' had outgrown its accommodation. The second shop from the left was that of John Wilde, a general draper, whose shop was called Manchester House. It is interesting that cotton sheets, pillow-cases and so on are still called 'Manchester goods' in Australia.

Gothic House, c. 1880. After demolition of Hawksworth's farm in 1868, Shuttleworth built his new double-fronted stationery and souvenir emporium in 1870. In addition to this successful enterprise he also had a newspaper stand at the station. Shuttleworth published, and printed, the *Ilkley Gazette* (price one penny) which he had founded in May 1861, and also published the *Wharfedale Almanac* and a popular guide book. He claimed to stock 10,000 photographs of Ilkley, Bolton Abbey, and other Yorkshire and English scenery. Gothic House is now occupied by Boots.

Brook Street looking south in the late 1870s. The conversion of the houses to shops on the east side has continued apace. The shops on the right with the protruding bay windows have been built next to Gothic House. The shop on the right hand corner is Hebblewhite's Boot and Shoe Shop established in 1875, where men's lace-up boots (for Sunday wear) could be bought for 9s 6d to 14s 6d while ladies button and lace boots (with Louis XV heels) could be had from 14s 6d. In the distance the spire of Wells Road Wesleyan church, built in 1876, can be seen. Behind the spire, White Wells beckons us towards the Moor.

Brook Street looking north, *c*. 1880. The tall building on the left was built for John Dobson, owner of the Troutbeck, in 1871. Next door is Wardle S. Bellerby's saddlery. The two-storey building is the original Station Hotel, while the small shop below this belongs to Joseph Moon, butcher. At the bottom of Brook Street note the Wheatsheaf (on the left) and old Star Inn.

Brook Street, *c*. 1886. The old thatch formerly occupied by Mr Shoesmith and most recently by Mr Campbell, is undergoing demolition to make way for the extension of the railway line. Moon's the butchers has moved to the corner of The Grove and the small shop is now occupied by Thomas Richardson, a boot maker. This shop, together with the Station Inn and Bellerby's shop, was subsequently demolished. The first shop beyond the demolition site is that of Matthew Sunderland, fishmonger and fruiterer. Immediately before the gable end advertisement for the *Ilkley Gazette* is the shop and gallery of Jesse Bontoft, the photographer, soon to be demolished to make way for new shops.

The Old Star and Wharfedale Inns, *c.* 1900. Both public houses were supplied by the Ilkley Brewery and Aerated Water Co., from their premises in Railway Road (now part of Spooners). The brewery, established in 1873, had its own spring supplying up to 7,000 gallons of water per hour 'eminently adapted for brewing purposes'. It produced the usual draught ales and stout, together with a bottled beer (Olicana) and a bottled Extra Stout for invalids containing 'all the strengthening and health-giving qualities of the finest English hops and malt…It has received very flattering encomiums from the medical faculty.'

Behind the Star, *c.* 1900. The side of the Star Inn adjoins William Ackroyd's, decorators and painters, while a narrow passage leading to the old gasworks separates these premises from the Wheatsheaf Hotel. The 'wheatsheaf' is derived from the old crest of the Middleton family. The hotel was functional rather than decorative and had a loyal clientele in the tap room, the so-called 'Pint-Pot Parliament'. The busiest time in the pub's calendar was Ilkley Feast week – on the Sunday up to 190 gigs and traps would be parked behind the Wheatsheaf adjacent to the site of the fair. The hotel was demolished in 1959 to create gardens around the church.

Ilkley town centre, 1900. This artist's impression gives a clearer picture of the layout of the foot of Brook Street. The Star and the Wharfedale Inns create a tight corner at the entrance to Leeds Road. Indeed there was a fatality at this junction in 1832 when a horse-drawn coach overturned and Hannah Allerton from Farsley was killed. Behind the Star is the chimney of the original gasworks. The drawing was prepared for the benefit of the town council who wished to remove the traffic hazard and provide a new office block by demolishing the two public houses and setting the building line as a continuation of Church Street.

Foot of Brook Street, c. 1906. The old Star and the Wharfedale were duly demolished but the prestigious office block did not materialize. Instead a new Star arose. The foundation of the new public house, to be known as The Star of Wharfedale, was laid in March 1905 on land at the rear of the original which had been cleared of outbuildings and part of the gasworks. Thanks to the energy of the builders, the pub was ready for occupation by September. Demolition of the two old inns then followed and the new Star was opened for business the following week. Such haste was a condition of maintenance of the licence, and no doubt met with the full co-operation of the regulars.

Brook Street, *c.* 1897. Before the changes at the foot of Brook Street came the extension of the railway to Skipton. The rail connection with Bradford and Leeds had been established on 1 August 1865, but Ilkley was not seen as the terminus of the line as it is today. In 1883 a Midland Railway's bill for a line to Skipton received the Royal Assent. The proposal caused a furore as the extension would split the town in two, however, work commenced in 1885 and the first passenger service to Bolton Abbey commenced in May 1888. By October trains were running through to Skipton. New buildings are also evident; the Bradford Old Bank (now Barclays) on the left dwarfs the hut belonging to Ellis Ingham, coal merchant and estate agent.

Planting trees in Brook Street, 1908. A typical British phenomenon – the three individuals carrying out the manual work are heavily outnumbered by spectators, including two gentlemen on the right who would pass for town councillors. The shops on the left are part of Brook Terrace, which has now been extended around the corner into Church Street. On the extreme left is Earnshaw's jewellers, then Ineson's, a hairdresser and tobacconist who obviously has a sideline in umbrella repairs, then Saunder's game and poultry and Charles Hutton, hatter and hosier.

Lower part of Brook Street from the corner of Railway Road, *c.* 1912. The street has now taken its final form. The building immediately behind the car was erected in 1892 following demolition of Bontoft's gallery. The corner site is occupied by the original Johnson's café and shop, where Ilkley Wells Toffee was available in souvenir tins. Interestingly, when the foundations were being dug for this building an ancient well was discovered in the bottom of which was a well preserved (sic) Roman pitcher. The comedian Albert Modley, who worked at the railway station, played the piano at Johnson's before embarking on a stage career.

Mott's Shop, *c.* 1936. Mott's were the best known occupants of the Gothic House shop in Brook Street after it was vacated by Shuttleworths in 1920. They began as cabinet makers and upholsterers but later went into china, for which they are best remembered. George Mott stands on the left with his two young assistants, the one on the right being Claude Daniels.

Beanlands' shop, c. 1937. Joseph Beanlands established a grocery shop in Railway Road in 1869 but this had to be demolished along with seventeen houses, two workshops and several stables when the road was diverted to make way for the new Skipton line platforms. He then moved to this corner site and a little later built the adjacent store in Railway Road. Its high arch was to allow the passage of horse-drawn delivery vans but by the time of this photograph horses had given way to ruby-coloured vans. Eventually the Beanlands brothers had shops in The Grove and at Ben Rhydding in addition to Brook Street. However they contracted in the 1950s and '60s down to one shop in the Arcade, but this closed in 1973.

The New Cinema, Railway Road 1937. For many years Ilkley boasted two cinemas; the New Cinema (later the Essoldo) and The Grove Picture House which was situated on Back Grove Road. The New Cinema (opened 1928) had a ballroom and café and had 'grand organ music at each performance'. In the 1930s the cinema manager, Mr Clough, was renowned for driving a Hispano Suiza car that once belonged to King Alfonso of Spain. The organist, Ernest Broadbent, was succeeded by Miss Frieda Hall in 1936. After the war Mr Gledhill played the organ while Bradley Hustwick and his Band hosted Saturday night dances. The cinema incorporated two shops; Kells Drapery Store and Maison Centrale, ladies hairdressers. It was demolished in 1969. Sunwin House now stands on the site.

Brook Street, *c.* 1958. The corner site was occupied by Percy Dalton's butchers shop. On the right of the street Woolworth's appeared in the 1930s. In the foreground a pre-war Ford 8 is still going strong.

The bridge comes down, 1966. The Ilkley-Skipton railway was closed under the Beeching cuts in March 1965. The railway bridge that dominated Brook Street for almost eighty years was demolished on Sunday 10 July 1966. Work started at 5 a.m. and despite the early hour a fair crowd gathered to see a giant mobile crane lower the big supporting arches into the road. The western abutment and the embankment that ran across what is now the central carpark had been removed, but it was several years before the eastern abutment was demolished. This occurred at the time of the station redevelopment in the 1980s.

Five
Church Street

Church Street looking east, c. 1880. The railings on the right belong to Box Tree Cottage, which was occupied by George Burton, a farmer and milk vendor. The white porch was part of the old vicarage, then occupied by William Burnell, a joiner. On the left John Naylor was a grocer, while the shop next door in a house built in 1709 (now the Mallard) belonged to John Waddington, a bootmaker. The tower of the parish church dates from the fifteenth century.

Bottom of Church Street, 1870. These premises are Lister's Refreshment Rooms with William Lister and his wife pictured. Next door are dilapidated stables while immediately behind is the dairyhouse adjoining Box Tree Cottage. This property was demolished in 1894 to be replaced by Beanlands' Arcade.

The Rose and Crown, c. 1870. This old pub was the main coaching inn for Ilkley, placed as it was on the Leeds-Skipton turnpike. Before the coming of the railway in 1865, several coaches served Ilkley. The Hark Forward was the coach involved in a fatality – blamed on a drunken driver, John Townsend, and it was replaced by the Commerce in 1833. This gave way to the British Queen, which left Leeds at 10 a.m. on Mondays, Wednesdays and Thursdays and arrived at the Rose and Crown two hours later. It returned to Leeds at 6 p.m. The fare was 4s for an inside seat and 2s outside. In 1842 another coach, the Union, operated from the Listers Arms to Leeds.

North side of Church Street, 1893. W. Cook, saddle and harness maker, also seems to be selling some bric-a-brac which has caught the attention of Mrs Lister of Overdale, and her daughter Norah. Behind them is the shop of John Keighley, seller of fish, fruit and poultry. Beyond the archway leading into Castle Yard are Hudson's refreshment rooms and Ilkley Brewery's Old Wine and Spirit Stores.

Church Street looking west, 1893. This splendidly bearded local worthy can maintain a pose that would be impossible in Church Street today! On the left, the porch of the soon to be demolished old vicarage is notable in that a former curate George Fenton would hand out medical advice and cheap remedies to the poor from this doorway, hence its name 't'old Charity Hole'. The thatch facing up Church Street was the home of Mr Butterfield's donkey business.

Church Street from outside the Listers Arms, *c.* 1900. John Keighley's shop (immediately before the entrance to Castle Yard) has been demolished and a tall, three-storey building erected in 1895. This houses A. Lister Hainsworth's six and a half-pence bazaar and servants' registry office, and Misses Bean and Hart's Riverdale Café. In more recent times it was partly occupied by Stones' Ice Cream Shop, where generous helpings of Mrs Minnie Stones' home-made ice cream covered with double cream could be obtained for 6d.

Top of Church Street, *c.* 1900. On the left corner is a butcher's shop belonging to Mr Charlesworth and next door, with Cadbury's chocolate signs in the windows, is Colburn's confectioners and refreshment rooms. A guide tells us that 'Miss Colburn's brown bread is a noted speciality, and also her potted beef.' Behind the girl is the upper of two gateways in the wall around the 'kirk garth' which was rebuilt and fitted with iron railings in 1849. The railings were removed during the Second World War.

Bottom of Church Street, 12 July 1900. Following a cloudburst over the Moor, a torrent of water swept through the town causing between £50,000 and £70,000 worth of damage to property, and one fatality – Alfred Brogden was killed by a roof collapse in his father's workshop in Chapel Lane. At one time water at the foot of Church Street stood 5 to 6 feet deep and caused flooding in Mrs Jane Waddington's Refreshment Rooms and in premises occupied by Mr Curwen and Lambert Thackray.

Church Street looking west, c. 1905. The old vicarage and adjacent properties have been demolished to make way for Beanlands' Arcade (1895) and new shops with houses above, seen on the left. The man with the apron is probably Mr Robert Thackray, a grocer and corn dealer. Mr Butterfield has given up the donkey business and the new owners of his cottage have had the roof slated.

Six
The Grove

Entrance to The Grove, 1893. The block of offices and shops on the left were built on the site of Hartley's farmhouse, around 1870, on land purchased in the first Middleton Land Sale in 1867. The Craven Bank (later Martin's Bank and now Abbey National) occupies the near corner. A further plot purchased in the same sale is occupied by the Congregational church, built in 1869. Beyond the church is the tower of the Spa Hydro. On the right hand corner carcasses of meat can be seen in Joseph Moon's shop, 'all killed and dressed on the premises'.

The Grove looking west, *c.* 1905. The handsome pair of shops with two tiers of bay windows was built in 1899. The nearer was occupied by Miss Procter, who had an artist's repository, and Miss Duxbury, a milliner. The other shop belonged to Fred Heap who sold an unlikely combination of pianos and bicycles. He was the only tuner in Ilkley.

The Grove looking west from the corner of Riddings Road, *c.* 1900. The wall and railings on the left surround the Congregational church while the shop on the extreme right (covered in ivy) is the low mock-Tudor building erected in 1884 by William Scott, artist and photographer. In 1900 he shared the property with the Imperial Café.

The north side of The Grove, c. 1910. The railings (to lean bicycles against) are outside the coffee and tea shop of the Imperial Café. This café and the Kiosk Café further down The Grove were both owned by C.E. Taylor & Co. of Harrogate, suppliers of Yorkshire Tea. Next door is Ellis Beanlands' grocery shop, followed by William Tomlinson, cabinet-maker and undertaker.

Upper rooms, Imperial Café, c. 1930. The café was a fashionable meeting place for Ilkley society. In the 1920s ladies from two of the three Ilkley millionaire families were regular customers. However the prices at that time seem ludicrously cheap; seven scones cost 3d, two pounds of sugar were 3d and a quarter pound of tea or coffee cost 8d – so you didn't have to be a millionaire. These rooms now form the upstairs part of Studio 68.

The Grove, c. 1910. The block of three shops with houses above were erected in 1877. The delicate cast-iron filigree balcony and canopy above were removed some years ago, although unlike a lot of cast iron work it did survive the Second World War. As for the shops, R.M. Green was a 'furnishing and building ironmonger', while next door was Thomas Vickers's newsagents and booksellers. The third shop was occupied by Henry Moisley, who sold boots and shoes.

The Grove looking east, c. 1900. Ladies promenade while a horse-drawn vehicle and a solitary horse rider constitute the only traffic.

The Grove looking east, 31 July 1912. On the extreme left with a giant tin of Horlicks on the pavement is Taylor's Drug Co. Ltd. Above this shop was Ilkley's first telephone exchange, the 'National Telephone Company's public call office and exchange'. The next shop (James Barron, glass and china dealer) has retained its railings marking that part of the pavement that belonged to the shop owners. The remainder of the pavement is owned by the council. To this day an uninterrupted line running down the middle of the pavement demarcates this dual ownership.

Detail of The Grove, 1912. Close inspection of the placards outside Vickers's newsagents reveals, with the help of a microscope, that the *Yorkshire Post* carries the story of the 'Titanic Inquiry'. The Government committee set up to investigate the loss of the *Titanic* delivered its report on 30 July 1912. The *Yorkshire Post* published an account of Lord Mersey's report on Wednesday 31 July thereby pinpointing the date.

The Grove looking east, *c. 1920*. A Model T Ford pick-up truck stands outside the shoe shop of Freeman, Hardy and Willis. Next door is the 'art needlework depot' of Misses Annie and Lilian Brownhill. The truck belonged to Mr Johnson, milkman of Church Street, whose premises (The Creamery) are now occupied by Dodd, Frankland, Stocks, next to Glover's showroom.

The Grove Ilkley.

The Grove looking east, *c. 1914*. On the left, the hedge and railings surround the Canker Well gardens at the corner with Cunliffe Road. This was originally called Pollard's Well after a seventeenth-century Ilkley blacksmith, Walter Pollard. The area was renovated in 1890. On the other corner of Cunliffe Road is the shop and house of Mr J.G. Boden, painter and decorator, built in 1898. The gateway on the right leads into the forecourt of the Spa Hydro.

The end of The Grove, north side, *c.* 1925. The Canker Well gardens have been opened out. The first house (Carlton House) has a long history as a doctor's residence and in recent years belonged to Dr T.B. Plummer. The building beyond the two sun-blinds was Ilkley's first town hall. The Local Board moved here in 1885 from offices above a shop in Brook Street. The Board became an Urban District Council in 1894 and in 1907 moved to the present town hall. The conservatory (now Brown's restaurant) belonged to Moffat's, the florists.

The Canker Well and Spa Flats, 1975. The spring issuing from the drinking fountain was a chalybeate source long famed for its tonic and healing properties. The water contained small quantities of iron, magnesia and lime. Unfortunately the supply was diverted and lost after house building across The Grove. The Spa was converted to flats in 1910. The building was demolished in 1989, and a new apartment block erected in the following year, but only after the builders had dealt with the spring that originally fed the well to be found at the rear! A single gate post remains at each end of the present forecourt.

The Grove, 1939. The wall around the Spa Flats has been replaced by a low chain and post fence, and the forecourt serves as a car park. The picture includes a fine array of pre-war cars including (from left to right), a Bentley, a Ford Model B, a Standard, and in the Spa car park, among others, a Morris 8 and a Rover 12 Sports saloon. However, parking along The Grove has not yet reached saturation point!

Seven

The Town Grows

Hangingstones quarry, c. 1880. The Victorian expansion of Ilkley relied almost entirely on local stone. Hangingstones Quarry, close to the Cow and Calf Rocks was the main source. The huge rocks were manoeuvred out of the quarry on sledges and brought down Hangingstones Road and Cowpasture Road by horse and cart to be taken to stone yards in Ash Grove and Ben Rhydding. The steep gradient necessitated much use of brakes. One local resident wrote to the paper complaining about 'the howling, creaking sound of their clumsy brakes.'

Looking north from above West View, 1867. Ilkley is in its infancy. Brook Terrace and the curve of the Crescent Hotel are evident. The mill dam and the upper mill are seen in the middle distance. At this time the former corn mill was being used as a saw mill. This ceased working in 1868, and the owner Thomas Lister moved to the newly erected Midland Hotel as manager.

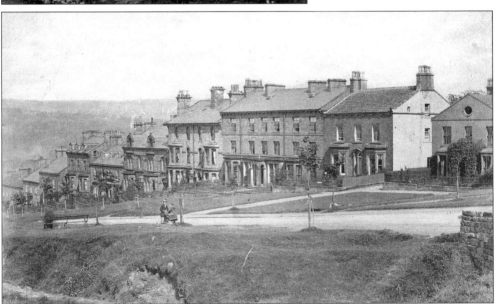

West View, c. 1890. West View was very much a part of the Heather Spa aspect of Ilkley. Apart from Moor Cottage on the right, the home of Mr W. Wormald, these properties were all given over to accommodation for visitors. Mrs Sagar let apartments in Moor Lodge, while the next building is Crescent House (now Rombalds Hotel) where Sarah Beanlands also offered apartments for rent. The diminutive trees allow an unusually unobstructed view of the houses.

Wells Road, 1893. The buildings on the right were erected in the wake of the 1867 land sale. The first block (now Dacre, Son and Hartley) was built around 1870. The walls, which are now covered in stucco, were built with distinctive cream-coloured bricks. The choice of building brick appears to have been dictated by the Middletons, as Charles was a major shareholder in the Tadcaster brickworks where they were made! A similar brick, in places still not rendered, was used for buildings on the The Grove. Further down, the lower stone building was occupied by a grocer, John Watkinson, and by J. Rhodes, an ironmonger, whose goods sprawl onto the pavement. The next building with the bay windows and iron railings was the post office. Beyond this was the confectionery shop of James Campbell. The projecting turret (and the spire behind) belong to the Wesleyan chapel.

West View, 1893. The lower part of West View was also given over to apartments for visitors. No. 3 was still occupied by the Usher family (Miss Elizabeth Usher), fifty years on from Dr Rischanek's stay at Usher's boarding house.

Wells Road, 1893. The Royal Hotel and its recently built annexe are on the left. The wall on the right surrounds the garden of the 'new' vicarage, built in 1848, which, after a further move of the vicarage, became Skelda Grange. The garden is now occupied by a row of town houses. The large building at the foot of the road was partly occupied by the Ilkley Library and Newsroom. Readers had to pay for the privilege of using this facility and throughout the 1890s there was much public agitation for a free library.

Post office staff and postmen, *c.* 1905. The first Ilkley post office was reputed to be in the old thatch in Green Lane and the postmaster was Thomas Stephenson. However, the earliest postal reference was in 1838 and by this time Richard Vickers was the postmaster. The office was situated in Eastgate (Leeds Road) until about 1850 when it moved to the White House just beyond the old grammar school in Addingham (Skipton) Road. Richard Vickers died in 1872 at the age of sixty-six and was succeeded by his sister Rebecca who carried out the duties of postmistress until 1884. William Vickers was then appointed postmaster and this probably coincided with the move to 12 Wells Road. He was followed by William Russell Stanley. Here the town's postmen, and telegraph boys, have assembled with the then postmaster, Mr M.A. Moffat (on the right in suit and tie). The post office building has been given a new ground-floor frontage since it was pictured in 1893 (see p. 65). The shop beyond the post office has changed ownership and belongs to Mr C.A. Broadhead, jeweller and silversmith, whose speciality was the Ilkley Souvenir Spoon made in solid silver. He claimed, no doubt with considerable pride, that his shop had been 'directly patronized' by Her Majesty Queen Alexandra, HRH The Duchess of Fife and Her Grace The Duchess of Devonshire. The post office moved from Wells Road to Chantry Drive in 1913 and from there to its present location at the station in 1989.

Foot of Wells Road, 1904. This site was occupied by the shop and office of John Green, a coal, coke and lime merchant, who established his business in 1840. He had coal stocks and loading bays at Addingham, Bolton Abbey and Grassington stations as well as at Ilkley. The buildings were demolished later in the year.

Foot of Wells Road, c. 1906. Demolition of John Green's premises made way for the handsome bank of the York City and County Banking Co. Ltd, which had outgrown premises at 46 The Grove. The bank was opened in 1905. It now belongs to the Midland (HSBC) Bank but the monogram YCCB can still be seen carved in stonework above the entrance.

Foot of Wells Promenade, *c.* 1910. On the extreme left is part of Roundell and Blackburn's confectionery shop; the middle shop belongs to Alfred Vickers who sold fancy goods as did The Jap stores on the corner. The latter shop belonged to Mr Knight who specialised in Japanese novelties. In 1912 these two shops on the right of the building were purchased by the London City and Midland Bank Ltd, who created a stone frontage with mullioned windows which remains today. The bank's heraldic shield still graces the Wells Promenade side.

Leeds Road looking east, *c.* 1905. The beginning of Leeds Road was occupied by the Crescent yard, Crescent Terrace and The Bay Horse public house on the right, and by a group of shops built in 1878 following the demolition of Collyer's old smithy. Further along the road we see on the right Walmsley's Ilkley Supply Stores selling groceries, wines and spirits, while directly ahead (behind the cyclist) are shops belonging to Dean Bros., builders and monumental masons, Mrs Dean, a fent dealer, and Mr Skillington, a painter and decorator.

Wellington Road, *c.* 1905. On the left hand corner is the shop of George Calvert, greengrocer and window cleaner. The sign informs us that the shop sells George Wroe's lime juice tablets at eightpence per pound. Across the road are the premises of Mason and Spencer, coal merchants and cab proprietors.

Children in Nelson Road, *c.* 1905. Most of these children appear to be in their Sunday best. The boys at the back are on stilts and seem to be standing fairly still! This particular postcard was very much a domestic affair. It was published by George Calvert of Wellington Road and posted to Miss Ethel Calvert at 46 Wellington Road, which is the address of Calvert's shop! Perhaps she is one of the children in the picture.

Clifton Terrace (Lower Wellington Road), *c.* 1912. A typical terrace of late Victorian houses complete with corner shop. Mr B. Robinson is a family grocer and wine and spirit dealer. The large house on the right held the offices of the Ilkley Gasworks which extended along Leeds Road to the right of Clifton Terrace (now the site of Booth's supermarket).

St James's Road, *c.* 1910. St James's and Oakburn Roads were laid out in the 1890s on a large field that lay north of One Oak and Oak House. The arrival of the photographer appears to have coincided with the presence of the postman (second right), the milkman (left), and a couple of house painters who have also joined the throng! The first collection from the new post box serving the area was at 5.15 p.m. on 3 June 1904.

Addingham (Skipton) Road, c. 1905. This row of houses opposite the end of Bolton Bridge Road was called West Terrace. The first house is Hawthorn Cottage, the home of George Smith, a builder and contractor. The man with the handcart may be connected with the business but the large brush in the cart suggests that he's more likely to be a road sweeper. The house at the end of the terrace, with an entrance to a yard at the back, belonged to Thomas Smith who was a joiner and undertaker.

Stubham Rise, c. 1912. This was the first group of new houses to be built across the river, at a time when the old bridge was still the main crossing point. The land was purchased in 1899 and the houses built by Dean Bros., from 1900 onwards. The name 'Stubham' has a long history, being mentioned in the Domesday Book. In the twelfth century, Hypolitus of Braham granted land at Follifoot, Stubham and Middleton to his second son Hugh. He and his descendants settled in Middleton and their first residence was Stubham Hall, Stubham being the southern part of Middleton township. This house was later called Low Hall.

Eight

People, Parades and Processions

The Army in Brook Street, *c.* 1905. Detachments of soldiers were frequent visitors to the town at the beginning of the century. This particularly splendid body of men, led by their band, marches through the town to their annual camp on one of the Holmes fields. The townspeople have turned out in large numbers to welcome them, no doubt the warmest welcome coming from the local tradesmen who were responsible for the supply of provisions.

Camp in West Holmes Field, c. 1912. Both the West and East Holmes were popular sites for army camps in the early 1900s. Here we see the tents of the University Officer Training Corps at their summer camp on the football ground. The structure to the right of the marquee was a small stand for football spectators. Behind the camp are Edwardian houses along Denton Road.

The Prince of Wales and his Ilkley Toffee, c. 1895. HRH The Prince of Wales has just accepted a tin of Ilkley Wells Toffee from the girl on the left. This clever piece of publicity was arranged by Mr W.A. Johnson of Johnson's Café, Brook Street, and took place when the Prince alighted from the royal train at Bolton Abbey Station. No doubt the toffee sustained him during the grouse-shoot with the Duke of Devonshire.

Funeral of King Edward VII, 30 May 1910. Solemn processions were held throughout the country to mark the passing of this popular King. The Ilkley procession, at this point made up of town dignitaries in their silk top-hats, passes in front of the station before turning down Brook Street on its way to the parish church. The procession was led by the Ilkley Brass Band and men of the 4th West Riding Howitzer Brigade. The large size of the crowd is to some extent attributable to the closing of all shops and places of business.

Empire Day at Myddelton Lodge, 1911. Empire Day was instituted in 1904 and was held on 24 May, the birthday of Queen Victoria. On this particular Empire Day, Mr and Mrs Kellett were hosts of a sale of work in aid of the Northern Police Orphanage and the Northern Police Convalescent Home. Two of the other notables pictured here are Mr Haliwell Sutcliffe the novelist who, along with Mrs Sutcliffe, opened the sale, and Mr E.P. Arnold Forster who presided over the event.

Coronation celebrations in Station Road, 22 June 1911. The Coronation of George V was an occasion for much rejoicing. A parade started from the town hall and here we see the end of the procession. On the left the Boy Scouts are followed by the town councillors and other notables and the tail is formed by the Royal Antediluvian Order of Buffaloes in their chains of office. The railway sidings and goods yard and the cabmen's shelter are behind (this is now the site of the bus interchange). The garden at the right was replaced by the building of the Winter Gardens in 1913.

Recruiting march, 1914. New recruits from Ilkley and the surrounding area march out of Leeds Road to pass down Church Street. The men have volunteered for the 9th Duke of Wellington's Regiment, who ran a recruiting campaign in the district soon after the outbreak of the First World War.

Peace celebrations, 19 July 1919. There was a mass meeting of children (and their parents) at the top of Brook Street, where special hymns were sung. The music was provided by the Municipal Orchestra and the singing was conducted by Mr Isaac Hirst, organist and choirmaster at the parish church. A procession followed at 3 p.m., a children's tea and an aged folk's tea at 4 p.m., at 5 p.m. sports and games on the Holmes were followed by entertainment and dancing into the evening and a fireworks display to finish.

Armistice Day Parade, 1926. A wet November Sunday in Wells Road. The parade is led by five policemen and the Ilkley Brass Band. The old comrades come next, followed by the town's volunteer firemen. The main body of marchers is the Ilkley Howitzer Battery of the West Riding Howitzer Brigade. Following on, and still in Station Road, are members of the town council and companies of Girl Guides and Boy Scouts.

The Black Hats versus White Hats Cricket Teams, 1891. The Ilkley Cricket Club dates from 1850 and for many years played on land behind the New Inn (Listers Arms). In 1877 the club had to move to a relatively remote field now occupied by the Lawn Tennis Club. The result of the move was that nobody came to watch the matches and the club sank deeper into debt. Bill Lister suggested a fund-raising 'scratch match' and this was held in 1879. In the following year the club moved back into town, to the ground behind the Crescent Hotel, and on 28 September 1880 the first Tradesman's Novelty Cricket Match was held to coincide with Ilkley Feast. In 1882 the two teams, each with about twenty players, distinguished themselves by donning black or white hats. In 1883 red and white roses were preferred, and there was a repeat of 'the war of the roses' in 1887. Since that year, however, the black and white hats have remained *de rigeur*. The two teams pose in front of the wall separating the cricket field from Railway Road. Across the road are the new arches and abutments of the Ilkley to Skipton railway extension. In 1892 a handsome silver cup was purchased by subscription among the tradesmen and offered for annual competition.

Match in progress, 1891. The back of Nelson Road formed the boundary while the large building behind (centre left) was the Victoria Hall where Ilkley's swimming baths were located (now Andrew Hartley's showroom). The field is now occupied by Nile, Trafalgar and Victory Roads. The novelty cricket competition ran without interruption until the Second World War when it lapsed and there was a gap for over thirty years before its return in 1978.

Collecting for the carnival, 1904. The Black and White Hat's match soon became connected with a carnival in aid of local charities. The first such fancy dress parade was held in 1885. However fund raising was not restricted to Carnival Day. Here a couple of well dressed collectors are seeking donations by touring the town with a barrel organ. The photograph was taken on 1 August and the donkey obviously needed a sun-hat!

Carnival procession, *c.* 1910. The procession is assembling outside the town hall prior to its progress through the town to the Holmes fields. The proceedings are under the scrutiny of the gentlemen in the foreground included among whom is the President of the Carnival, Revd F. Sinker MA, vicar of All Saints.

Carnival procession, *c.* 1910. The procession has spread out somewhat on its route along The Grove and Bolton Bridge Road and the participants are heavily outnumbered by the spectators gathered across Skipton Road and at the end of Lister Street. The female spectators are in carnival mood, displaying a wonderful array of floral hats.

Carnival procession, 1933. The procession has obviously been re-routed since the earlier photographs and now proceeds in an anti-clockwise direction! The parade is passing along The Grove at the junction with Riddings Road. The shops in the background are: Broadbent's bookshop, Crockatt's dyers and cleaners, and Dinsdale's wine and spirit merchants. Dinsdale's took over two adjacent shops in 1898 and converted them into one. During the conversion they created two mosaics in the entrances, each featuring the monogram D&Co. These mosaics are still present in the entrances to The Grove Bookshop and the Cancer Research Campaign shop next door. The latter also has a bunch of grapes carved in the door panel, a reminder of its former connection with the wine trade.

Jubilee carnival procession, 1935. There was a particularly ambitious carnival procession in May 1935 to mark the Silver Jubilee of King George V. The parade of decorated lorries has just set off from the town hall. The second vehicle belonged to Mr William Petty who had a haulage business in the old Brewery Yard. In the background is Peggy's café, a well known place of refreshment, while the other corner is occupied by Eva Kitson's confectionery shop. In addition to the parade, there was a swimming gala in Ilkley's newly opened pool, sports competitions and a free tea for all.

Carnival and cricket, 1936. A happy group of Black and White Hats players and carnival participants pose on the East Holmes. Up to 1934 only men took part in the cricket match but in that year the teams became mixed. By 1937 a woman had risen to captaincy – the White Hats being captained by Miss P. Wellen – however, the Black Hats won.

Ilkley Sheep Fair, 1898. The annual sheep fair was held on land at the back of the Wheatsheaf Hotel (where the funfair associated with Ilkley Feast was held) and on land opposite the post office in Wells Road, now occupied by the Christian Science church. The sale attracted farmers and dealers from throughout the dale and there were good numbers of Scotch lambs, half-bred lambs, 'lonks' (a dialect term for large sheep) and half-bred sheep for which to bid.

Nine

Buildings, Bridges and some Barrels!

Semon Convalescent Home, 1900. Charles Semon was a wealthy Bradford merchant who was Mayor of Bradford in 1865. He built the convalescent home that carried his name at a cost of £12,000. It opened in 1874 and Semon presented the home to Bradford Corporation in 1876, together with an endowment of £3,000. The home was 'to be used exclusively for persons of slender means whether born in the United Kingdom or elsewhere, and whether resident in Bradford or not, who are in a weak state of health, or who, having been ill, are tardily recovering and require for complete restoration to health good food, rest and kind treatment together with medical supervision'. In the 1880s and '90s the medical attendant was Dr Johnstone and he was followed by Dr Call. In 1912 the charge for admission was 12s 6d per week, payable in advance. The home served the community well for over 100 years before its recent closure and demolition.

Ilkley Museum, *c.* 1895. The museum building had been erected as a Methodist chapel in 1834. The building was vacated by the Methodists in 1869 and went through several changes of ownership, including use by the Salvation Army, before being purchased by the Museum Committee for £360 in 1891. It was opened as the town's first museum by Robert Collyer on 25 August 1892. Herbert Oxley, a chemist, was appointed as the first curator. The museum was taken over by the council in 1896. In May 1908 it was moved to an upper room in the new library and in 1961 to the Manor House.

Glover's garage, 1973. The structure of the old Methodist chapel and the original portico are clearly seen. The building was sold by the Urban District Council to Mr Charles Thackray in 1913 who established his Central Garage there. Mr Thackray served in the war and during his absence the garage was managed by his wife. It is strange to see the petrol pumps on the pavement in Bolton Bridge Road. Earlier, petrol was obtained through a gantry which swung out over the road, and kept the pavement clear for pedestrians. The garage was sold in 1937 to Harry Glover and to the present owner, Paul Bourgeois, in 1980.

Laying the foundation stone of the new town hall, 31 January 1906. During the 1890s the council were becoming increasingly dissatisfied with the accommodation in The Grove and there was much wrangling over the site for a new town hall. In March 1897 the present site was purchased at a cost of £6,270 from Mr J.T. Jackson, who just happened to be chairman of the Town Hall Committee. He had purchased the plot, previously occupied by a farmhouse – Sedburgh House, together with the West Holmes field in July 1896 for £7,800. The gentleman laying the stone is, of course, Mr J.T. Jackson.

Building in progress, January 1907. The crosses on the photograph indicate where scaffolding has collapsed sending two men to their death. The writer of the postcard, a Mr H. Sargeant, was an eye-witness. 'I send you this p.c. of the accident it was a sad affair it was the last stone to go up the two men were badly smashed I did what I could but it was no use I was sorry that I could not get to the ball owing to the fog...' The writing makes up in immediacy for what it lacks in grammar!

Ceremonial key presented to Dr Collyer, 2 October 1907. The opening of the library and town hall was something of a piecemeal affair. Robert Collyer was over from America to receive an honorary degree at Leeds University – a D.Litt., hence Dr Collyer, so he was invited to open the library. Unfortunately the building wasn't finished, but he declared it open anyway and received this key and an illuminated address. His association with the building is also evidenced by the presence of a bust to be seen, along with one of Carnegie, at the library entrance. Both were the work of Frances Darlington, a local sculptor. This was to be Collyer's last visit to Ilkley, he died in 1912, eight days before his eighty-ninth birthday. The town hall was opened on 27 April 1908 and the first council meeting in the new chamber was held on 6 May 1908.

The town hall, c. 1910. The town hall with its flanking library and assembly hall (but not yet the Winter Gardens) was designed by a Leeds architect, William Bakewell, who won an open competition that attracted sixty entries in 1903. The estimated cost was £13,000. Furnishing the town hall cost an additional £3,900. The American benefactor Andrew Carnegie donated £3,000 towards the provision of a free library. By August 1907 building of the town hall was well advanced and the clock was set in motion at 5 p.m. on the 31 August. The bell that strikes the hours weighs 5 cwts.

Auxiliary Military Hospital No. 1, Ilkley, 1917. The Convalescent Hospital was used as a military hospital during the First World War. It was opened in 1862 under the auspices of the Ilkley Bath Charitable Institution founded in 1829 by the curate George Fenton, to provide treatment for the poor, and was Yorkshire's first charity hospital. Subscribers paid 21s per year and this enabled them to nominate a person for three weeks stay at the hospital. The building, with a capacity of 70 beds, was smaller than at present and cost £3,016 including fittings. In 1885 the hospital was enlarged at a cost of £2,960 so that up to 100 patients could be accommodated. In 1886 the name was changed to the 'Ilkley Hospital and Convalescent Home'. At the outbreak of the First World War the hospital was commandeered for military use and in 1914 the horror of the war became apparent to the citizens of Ilkley when the first party of 62 wounded Belgian soldiers arrived by train. The group was met by the chairman of the council and taken by private cars to the hospital. Many people turned out to cheer the soldiers and provide them with cigarettes, sweets and money. As the war progressed they were followed by hundreds of our own men and women. At the news of the signing of the Armistice on 11 November 1918, the wounded soldiers took possession of a tradesman's dray and drove around the town making merry. They broke into the Volunteer Bugle Band's room in Bridge Lane and, after 'borrowing' some drums and bugles, led an impromptu parade through the streets. In the evening, after the soldiers had been persuaded to go back to the hospital, the parade was continued by the official Bugle Band who had by then retrieved their instruments.

Ilkley Hospital and Convalescent Home, c. 1935. This is the women's rest room which overlooked The Grove. A group of patients pursue their occupational therapy with Sister and Matron looking on. Between 1913 and 1929 the Matron was Miss S.E. Mather; she was succeeded in 1929 by Miss L. Hamlett who had been a Sister at the hospital for two years prior to her appointment. The hospital closed a few years ago and the site is now undergoing redevelopment by the Abbeyfield Society.

Ardenlea, Queens Drive, c. 1890. Ardenlea was built in 1881 for Mr and Mrs George Thorpe to the designs of the Bradford architect, T.C. Hope. Here members of the Thorpe family prepare to depart for an afternoon's excursion. Ardenlea subsequently became the Railwaymen's Convalescent Home and in 1963 the Marie Curie Home.

Railwaymen's Convalescent Home, Ardenlea, *c.* 1925. The house was purchased by the North Eastern Railway Company in 1914 and fitted out as a Convalescent Home. It was opened by the general manager of the company, Sir A. Kaye Butterworth on 8 May 1915. The home was not restricted to employees of the NER. Workers from the other great trunk railways as well as representatives of the smaller companies such as the London Electric Railway and the Welsh railways were admitted – as long as they paid a halfpenny per week into the Sickness Fund when they were working.

Railwaymen at Ardenlea, 23 July 1919. The presence of the 'policeman' and the 'pickpocket' give a clue to events leading up to this photograph. A favourite pastime at the home was the mock trial, when real or imagined misdemeanours by the patients were subjected to public scrutiny. 'The prisoners are defended by counsel appointed from amongst the guests by reason of their eloquence and the cases are decided upon by a jury guaranteed to be free from bias of every kind.' The maximum fine was a penny, so no fortunes, or tempers, were lost.

Heathcote, in the present day. Arguably the finest house in Ilkley, Heathcote was built in 1906 to the designs of Edwin Lutyens. It was built for Mr J. Hemingway, a textile manufacturer, at an estimated cost of £17,500. In order not to compete with the architectural features of the house, Lutyens insisted on designing all the furniture, hangings, curtains and carpets. His ideas were not always in tune with Hemingway's. Mr Hemingway asked for a wooden staircase but got a black marble one – according to Lutyens 'black lends dignity to decoration'. Mrs Hemingway, a former mill-girl, outlived her husband for many years and lived at Heathcote until 1936. Twenty years later the house was acquired by the N.G. Bailey Organisation for use as offices.

The new retort house, Ilkley Gasworks, 1935. From the sublime of Heathcote, to the strictly functional of the monolithic gas retort house. All the gas for the district was produced in this building at the Leeds Road gasworks until the 1960s. Thereafter the town's supply was provided by the national gas grid and subsequently in 1971 by natural (North Sea) gas. The gasworks site was gradually cleared and is now the site of Booths supermarket. The first gasworks was erected in 1857 behind the old Star Inn by the Ilkley Gas Light Company. There was an economical approach to street lighting in those early days; the lamps were extinguished four days before, and four days after, a full moon, and were not lit at all between April and September. With increasing gas distribution to businesses and private houses the original plant became inadequate and the works moved to the Leeds Road site in the 1870s. The company was purchased by the Local Board in 1893 for £35,000, at which date there were 847 customers on the books.

Hadfield Farm, c. 1914. Ilkley had numerous farms in the Victorian era. Hadfield Farm was owned by the Park family with the first mention of Mr Ridsdale Park as the occupant being in 1887. At that time the farmhouse comprised some old cottages on Skipton Road in an area of Ilkley called Wood Rhydding. By 1904 the farm had passed to Risdale's son Joseph Park and it was he who built the farmhouse and outbuildings some distance from the road.

Mr Park and his men, c. 1905. The men are making hay, no doubt while the sun shines. Haymaking involved strewing, turning and windrowing (laying in two overlapping rows) to allow the grass to dry. It was then 'led' into the barn using a horse-drawn hay-sweep and sledges, and 'forked up' into the hay-loft. All this labour merited a celebration when the hay was in. A 'mell' – harvest supper – sometimes followed by games, brought this annual effort to a welcome conclusion. Hadfield Farm was bought in 1917 by Mr Harry Ellis whose brother William Edward lived at Hollin Hall, and from 1959 was occupied by the Wallbanks. The farm was sold recently and the buildings are undergoing conversion into separate houses.

River Wharfe in flood, 1899. In January 1899 a period of sustained heavy rain was followed by extensive flooding in the Wharfe valley. At Addingham, work had to be suspended at Lister's Mill because the water was 8 feet above the normal level. Downriver at the suspension bridge a tree became entangled in the ironwork and, in attempting to remove it, an Ilkley man was swept away and drowned.

Ben Rhydding Toll Bridge, c. 1905. The Ben Rhydding bridge was built in 1882 and at that time was the only bridge between the Old Bridge in Ilkley and Otley Bridge, although there were fords, stepping stones and a ferry pulled across by a wire in Wheatley. A toll had to be paid to cross the bridge and the toll keeper's hut can be seen at the right hand end. The bridge was purchased by Ilkley UDC from the executors of Mr Arthur Hill in 1948.

Official opening of the new bridge, June 1906. The building of the new bridge was prompted by the development of Middleton by the Wharfedale Estate Co. It was first envisaged in 1899 but part of the land required in the West Holmes was occupied by Mr Horseman's nursery garden and the company had to wait a further three years for the lease to expire. The bridge, which cost £17,000, was opened by Cllr J.A. Middlebrook, Chairman of the Council. The ceremony was held late in the day so that the soldiers of the 3rd Lancashire Royal Volunteers could be the first to officially cross the bridge.

New Brook Street, 1912. The effect of the new bridge and the Middleton land sales on house building across the river is now evident. However, the only wheeled traffic is a hand-cart laden with ladders, pushed by an energetic window cleaner.

Pontoon bridge across the Wharfe, *c.* 1900. Here are the beer barrels! This old lantern slide is something of a mystery – at least to me. The temporary bridge appears to be conducting pipes across the river but the purpose remains obscure. The houses being built in the background are in Stubham Rise, this information both dates the picture and fixes the location a little downriver from the Old Bridge.

The Stepping Stones, *c.* 1905. A more conventional way to cross the river! These old stones are situated near Wheatley Lane and allow the intrepid pedestrian to cross to near Carters Lane. The stones were originally put in place to serve three cottages (long since gone) on the north side of the river. In 1875 Mr Middleton declined to renew some of the stones because, he argued, it gave poachers and other miscreants easy access to his land. The Local Board pressed the squire because the stepping stones formed part of a popular circular walk and he relented. Five of the stones were replaced in recent years after complaints that the crossing was becoming a gymnastic, and dangerous, exercise.

Ten
Transport of Delight

Mr. Jackson and his Donkeys, Ilkley.

Shuttleworth, Ilkley

'Donkey' Jackson, 1902. John 'Donkey' Jackson was born in a low thatched cottage on the east side of Brook Street and in adulthood became a woolcomber. However he gave up this trade and entered the transport business. He initially bought a mule and carriage but then purchased William Rigg's donkey business which he maintained for thirty-eight years.

Bridge Lane, 1893. On the left is Donkey Jackson's old cottage. Although the cottage was demolished around 1900, the steps leading up to the doorway are still there, opposite the workroom of Glover's garage. In 1897 the roof of Jackson's cottage collapsed and he had to move into Castle Yard. He died on 17 January 1907 at the age of eighty-one, leaving a widow and seven children, and Ilkley lost one of its most colourful characters.

Butterfield's cottage, 1867. Jackson's main (indeed only) rival for the donkey trade was Thomas Butterfield. He operated from this old thatch which stood looking onto an open piece of land at the foot of Church Street – where Pawson's Cottages are now.

Horse-drawn cabs at the top of Brook Street, *c.* 1910. The main stand of cabs was to be found for many years down the centre of Brook Street. There was another stand at the station. The fares were fixed by the Local Board; a one horse conveyance for four persons from Brook Street to Grove Road was 1s, to Wells House was 1s 6d, and to Ben Rhydding was 3s. Speaking at the Cabmen's Dinner in 1898, Revd J.H. Kempson declared that 'it will be a long time before the motor car has any effect on the cabmen of Ilkley'.

The cabmen's shelter, 1973. The driver of the horse-drawn cab had an unenviable existence, available for hire at all times and in all weathers his only refuge was one of the pubs – giving rise to a frequently undeserved reputation for insobriety. London philanthropists formed the Cabmen's Shelter Fund in 1874 to finance the provision of permanent structures for rest and refreshment. Provincial towns followed suit. The Ilkley shelter was removed intact in 1973 and taken to Embsay Station where it serves as the ticket office.

Ingle's smithy, Railway Road, c. 1885. In the heyday of horse-drawn transport there were several blacksmiths in Ilkley. The man in the leather apron is James Ingle who occupied this smithy before its demolition and the diversion of Railway Road, necessitated by the new railway lines to Skipton. A horse is being shod, and a plough is awaiting repair. James Ingle had three sons, Harold, Ernest and Reginald (Jim). Reginald brought the first commercial vehicle into Ilkley, an AC delivery 'tricycle', which he drove up from the AC works in Thames Ditton, a journey that took four days! The vehicle was used by Beanlands' on The Grove. It was not sold until the late 1950s when it was shipped to the USA by Roy Cunliffe Motor Cycles.

The cab stand at the station, c. 1900. The station was the original terminus of the Ilkley and Otley Joint Railway, an enterprise sponsored by the North Eastern and Midland Railways. The station was built by Israel Thornton at a cost of £2,770 on land purchased from the Trustees of Sedbergh School for £2,785. The first train left Ilkley for Leeds on 1 August 1865.

The staff at Ilkley Station, *c.* 1870. The staff are assembled on platform one. The picture looks unusual because it was taken prior to the installation of the glazed roof inside the station. James Nicholson, the stationmaster (seen with mutton chop whiskers and beard, wearing a bowler hat) served at the station from 1865 until 1906. In 1865 he was paid £160 per annum. A porter was paid 17s per week and the cleaner 5s.

The station, Ben Rhydding, *c.* 1905. Little of the station is visible, most of it being obscured by Wheatley Hall on the left. A train is approaching the bridge over Wheatley Lane.

Ben Rhydding Station, 1950s. The station was erected at the behest of Ben Rhydding Hydro. There would have been no other commercial reason to build a station so close to Ilkley to serve the hamlet of Wheatley. The name of the station began to be associated with the local area, which therefore became 'Ben Rhydding' and the original 'Wheatley' is only remembered in the road names and the hotel. The station was initially a small wooden structure, but Dr McLeod considered this inappropriate and, in 1871, spent £200 putting up the stone buildings we see here.

Easby Drive, c. 1905. The extension of the railway to Skipton necessitated the building of embankments, a viaduct and several bridges, including this one across Easby Drive. These structures were removed in 1973 a few years after the closure of the line.

Taxis at the top of Brook Street, *c.* 1914. The 1898 prediction that horse-drawn vehicles had a long future was soon disproved and after 1910 the internal combustion engine quickly gained the upper hand. The taxi nearest to the camera is a 'Unic'. The first taxi in Ilkley was driven by Mr Harry Roe, but it is not possible to confirm that this is his vehicle.

Private car in Skipton Road, *c.* 1910. This splendid car (an open-drive landaulette) of French origin, probably a Unic, complete with chauffeur stands at the junction of Lister Street and Skipton Road.

Denby and Co., motor engineers, 1925. Arthur Denby started a motorbike and cycle shop at 20 Leeds Road (now the Motor Spares shop) and lived above the premises. Walter Robinson joined as a partner and they opened the garage in Little Lane. Arthur Denby was a qualified engineer and built cars of his own design at this garage. The cars were exported in kit form via Ilkley railway goods depot. Standing outside are Dan Smith (a bus driver), Harry Walker (who after the Second World War founded Allen and Walker's electrical shop at the foot of Chantry Drive) and Jackie 'Tapwasher' Barnes who worked for the council.

Parkinson's limousine, 1927. Mr Bert Russell and Mr George Parkinson (on the right) stand proudly by a Rolls Royce Silver Ghost, which dates from around 1912, at the top of Brook Street. Mr Parkinson was the proprietor of the West Riding Motor Company, located in the Grand Garage in Railway Road. The Rolls, together with Austin Landaulettes, were available for hire 'at very reasonable terms' while the garage would supply 'any make of new car or motor cycle'.

An 'early' bus, 1927. Mr Parkinson (on the left) has walked round from Brook Street into Railway Road to be included on this photograph as well. On the right is Mr P. Stirk of Addingham, the driver. The bus is a Commer, a popular bus-chassis in its day. It is parked outside a smithy that was taken over by James Ingle when his original smithy (see p. 98) was demolished. This is now the site of Sunwin House.

Arthur Green's shooting brake, *c.* 1947. This splendid shooting brake (estate car) was converted from a pre-war Bentley saloon for Mr Arthur Green by Chambers Bros, who had their garage in Castle Road close to the new bridge. The newly painted car stands outside Chambers' paint shop awaiting collection. The colour scheme, orange and black, was highly unusual for post-war times when cars were either black or dark monochrome green or ruby. However, this was an early example of using corporate colours. Arthur Green had a timber business and all his timber lorries, cars and other vehicles were painted in the same colour scheme. The garage and the adjoining house were demolished in the 1970s.

Bus in Springs Lane, 1931. The garage belonged to Mr Claude Scott who later moved to the Station Garage further along the road (recently demolished). Scott's garage adjoined Sidney Lancaster's boot repairers and housed Thomas Pepper's horse and cart. Mr Pepper was a carrier contracted to the London Midland and Scottish Railway and had facilities in the Station Yard, but the carter was Mr Dalton who was only retired in 1955 when a motor vehicle took over!

Bus in Hangingstone Road, 1932. This bus (a Leyland Royal Tiger) provided the Moor Top Service, taking visitors from the town centre up to the Cow and Calf Rocks during the summer months. Prior to the advent of motor traffic, Hangingstone Road was little more than a quarry road. It continued past the Highfield Hotel (later Cow and Calf Hotel) and Highfield House as a poorly-maintained lane to Burley Woodhead, but the route was little used by horse-drawn vehicles because of the steep gradients.

West Yorkshire bus, Brook Street, July 1932. The bus is a fifty-three seater Leyland Titan. Three well known shops are identifiable. On the corner of The Grove is Percy Dalton's butchers shop ('Pickled Beef and Tongues always on hand'); next door is Boots The Chemists with its once familiar sign, and then Ernest W. Busby's fashion shop, who had a further branch of his business in Kirkgate, Bradford.

Bus in Brook St, 1932. The bus, a Leyland, is heading for Huddersfield via Bradford. Ingham's huge sign points to a diminutive wooden hut nestling between Barclay's Bank and the railway bridge. On the right, Mrs Annie Wilkinson's shop sold fruit and vegetables. She also had a flower shop in the Station Approach. The shop with the sunblind is Austin Dobson's tobacconists. Mr Hampshire across the street sold fish, fowl and fruit. He was so polite that he would raise his bowler hat when answering the telephone to one of his esteemed lady customers!

Bus traffic outside the Constitutional Club, July 1932. Two Leyland buses negotiate the corner on their way in and out of The West Yorkshire Road Car Company bus-depot at the junction of Cunliffe Road and South Hawksworth Street (now the Moors Centre). The Constitutional Club and the Freemasons occupy a building erected and originally owned by Messrs Dean Brothers who gave the club a ten-year lease at £85 per annum. The official opening, held on 28 August 1897, was performed by the Rt. Hon. Akers-Douglas assisted by the constituency MP, Mr D'Arcy Wyvill. The £85 rent remained unaltered until August 1917, but the ravages of the First World War greatly depleted the membership and the club ran into serious debt. The card room was given up, the Steward was 'released' and the landlords were persuaded to reduce the rent to £60 per annum. However, in August 1919 the Dean Brothers served a notice on the club to quit or purchase the building for £1,400. The club approached a wealthy member, Mr J.T. Hemingway of Heathcote, who suggested an offer of £1,100 but eventually provided £1,350, a sum acceptable to the Deans. Purchase was completed on 1 December 1919. Not unexpectedly, Mr Hemingway became club president in 1920 and served in this office until 1926.

Eleven
Schools and Scholars

Old Grammar School, Ilkley, 1869.

Shuttleworth, Ilkley

Old grammar school, Skipton Road, 1869. Around 1600 an Ilkley man, George Marshall, left £100 'for some godly and charitable uses'. In 1607 this was employed to practical effect, 'the sum of £100 shall for ever hereafter be employed towards the maintenance of a schoolmaster of a Grammar School at Ilkley'. A generation of children were taught in the church before the opening of the school building in 1637. In the early Victorian era there were two teachers, John Robinson and John Hobson. Mr Robinson was a strict disciplinarian but Hobson suffered from the fact that he was knock-kneed and the children invariably referred to him as 'Knocking Johnny'. He lived in the old vicarage in Church Street. Following the Schools' Inquiry Commission visit of 1866, Mr Fitch the Assistant Commissioner reported that 'the Vicar (Revd John Snowdon) is nominally the headmaster. He does not teach, however, but pays £50 per annum to the assistant, Thomas Wood' (seen standing in the doorway). In 1867 Mr Martin the Inspector of Charities visited Ilkley and following his report on the school, the Church Commissioners proposed that it should be re-established with the schoolmaster independent of the vicar.

The 'new' grammar school, c. 1900. Although a scheme for the building of a new school was proposed in 1872, there then followed a prolonged period of dispute and debate. There was discord over the sources of money, the size and character of the school and a suitable site. In the meantime the pupils were absorbed into the National Schools in Leeds Road that opened in 1872. It was not until 1881 that the site was purchased, for £2,420, and a further ten years of wrangling followed before building was commenced in 1892. The headmaster, Mr Frederick Swann, was appointed in April 1893 and the school opened in September.

Ilkley Grammar School Sports Day, c. 1905. The judges are clustered around the long jump on a cold and windy day. Until 1904 the school did not have its own playing fields but in that year Mr Swann arranged the purchase of the field in Ben Rhydding for £1,000 which worked out at 10 pence per square yard, a very good bargain for the school. A pavilion was erected in 1905 and served the players and officials until its demolition in 1963. The field is now the site of the IWS building which was opened in 1968.

Old scholars, 1955. About ninety 'old boys' of Ilkley Grammar School attended this dinner held at the Crescent Hotel. The retiring president of the Old Olicanians, Mr Jimmy Reed, handed over the office to Mr Tommy Walker. The principal guest was Sir James Croysdale, Lord Mayor of Leeds – also an Old Olicanian. Three of those present had been pupils during the headship of Mr Swann, who left the school in 1904. They were unquestionably the oldest old boys.

Young scholars, c. 1932. Primary children in Miss Shackleton's class at Ben Rhydding Council School. This was an all-age school taking pupils from five to fourteen years, and was under the control of the old West Riding Education Committee. In recent years the school became Bolling Road First School.

The High School for Girls, Wells Road, *c.* 1906. Ilkley had a multitude of small private schools at the end of the Victorian era. Most were established in large houses and usually had a short life span. The high school was typical of this educational proliferation and was situated at this time in Annandale, the former home of Dr Thomas Johnstone, physician to Ben Rhydding and several other establishments. Earlier the high school had been housed in Holme Lea. It was run by the Misses Rhodes and later by Miss Thorpe, and was a forerunner of Moorfield School. Other schools for girls at this time were the Ladies College in Belle Vue; Crossbeck House run by Misses Marian and Fanny Patterson; Glendair, Briardene and Oaklands.

Clevedon House School, *c.* 1910. The school was 'transplanted' from Woodhall Spa in Lincolnshire to Ilkley in 1905 following the purchase of Wharfedale Grange. The first (joint) headmasters were Mr Dean and Mr Stokoe. In 1928 the school was purchased by Mr Frank Kidson in partnership with an old friend from his Sedbergh School days, W.W. Wakefield (later Lord Wakefield of Kendal) who played rugby for England. Mr Kidson presided over the golden age of the school. It grew substantially during the Second World War and by 1952 had sixty-four pupils. Mr Kidson retired in 1965. The school was taken over by the Licensed Victuallers in 1982.

Oaklands School, North House, c. 1930. Oaklands School for girls was one of Ilkley's longer lived establishments. It started in a private house (the original Cherry Bank) in Queens Road in 1896 and expanded into a second house off Westwood Drive in 1920. During the 1920s and '30s the school was in the charge of Miss Clague and Miss Perry, and in 1943 was taken over by Mr and Mrs W. Saville. The school then enjoyed a twenty year period of stability and success, but a swift decline in the early '60s led to its closure in 1965.

The gymnasium, Oaklands School, c. 1950. 'Girls are encouraged to cultivate a taste for the natural and unaffected rather than the artificial, and to equip themselves to play a useful part in life'. This ethos was pursued through sports and gymnastics, walks on the Moors, and uniformed organisations – the school had its own Girl Guide and Brownie companies. There was accommodation for sixty resident pupils and day pupils were also taken. The fees in 1954 for board, residence and instruction were 57 guineas per term for girls under twelve, and 60 guineas for the over twelves.

Heathfield School, Westwood Drive, *c.* 1920. Heathfield was built for Mr George W. Brown in the 1890s. It was then occupied by the Harvey family before becoming Heathfield School. The school closed in 1942 and became Moorland House ('naughty boys') School.

Tennis courts, Heathfield School, *c.* 1920. Gymslips and lisle stockings had to be worn at all times – even for tennis!

The Deaconess College, *c*. 1905. This building in Queens Road was erected as a boys' boarding school – Ilkley College, in 1869. It was built by the first principal, Mr Edward Sewell, at a cost of £15,000. A gymnasium and lecture hall was added in 1874. In 1877 it was described as 'one of the prettiest buildings in Ilkley, picturesque in outline, and effectively broken by gables and dormers and a castellated tower of five storeys commanding a view of one hundred square miles of the most beautiful scenery to be found in England'. In the 1890s there was accommodation for sixty boys. In 1902 the building was purchased by the Wesley Deaconess Order as its teaching headquarters. The Order was founded in 1890 in London by Revd Dr Thomas Bowman Stephenson, a remarkable man who also founded the National Children's Homes. Stephenson saw a need for women to work in cities and towns in a way that combined pastoral care with evangelism. Women could go where men would not be welcomed, many families needed nursing and practical help. To carry out this role the deaconesses undertook one or two years training. Stephenson moved the Order to Ilkley when he became Minister of the Ilkley Wesleyan (Wells Road) church. The college closed in Ilkley in 1968 and the building was converted into flats – Deaconess Court.

The resident staff and trainee deaconesses, *c.* 1910. The warden, Revd William Bradfield and Mrs Bradfield sit in the centre. Other members of staff, in darker uniforms, are Sister Emily Orr (tutor), Sister Louise Homer (home sister), Sister Esther Taylor (secretary), and Sister Hilda Marris (organising secretary). There were twenty-two students at this time. Deaconesses pledged to remain single with the intention of a life of service to the church. However in 1965 the Methodist Conference accepted that a deaconess who married could remain a member of the Order 'if she so desires and is willing to accept the discipline of the order'.

Prayer room, Deaconess College, *c.* 1930.

Twelve
Churches and Chapels

All Saints church, 1904. Christianity was first brought to the northern Anglo-Saxons by St Paulinus who baptised King Edwin of Northumbria in AD 627. In the five years that followed Paulinus and his assistants preached the gospel throughout the North, principally in the towns established by the Romans. Their travels must have brought them along the Roman roads to Ilkley where the British inhabitants might already have been under the sway of Christianised Anglo-Saxons. It certainly seems reasonable to date the arrival of Christianity in Ilkley to this early missionary period. The Domesday Book (1085) mentions 'a church and a priest' at Ilkley. The latter detail is interesting because one of the few tangible links we have with the Norman period is the fine archway with its tooth-work ornamentation over the main door. The most noteworthy change since 1904 is the removal of the graves and grassing of the former graveyard. A few headstones were retained adjacent to Church House, including that of Harriet Collyer, Robert's first wife who died in childbirth. The remainder are stacked up in the corner of the cemetery.

Saxon crosses, *c.* 1880. These three crosses date from the Anglian period and are evidence of a church well before the Norman Conquest. The tallest shaft is dated to about AD 850, it has subsequently been fitted with a cross-head, found in two parts, which does not belong to it. The lower part of the head had been kept at Myddelton Lodge and the upper part was found in the river in 1884. The next tallest shaft is very worn and defaced having been used as a gatepost at some time. The shortest stone is the upper part of a large cross and is of an earlier style than the other two, dating from before AD 800. The stones were lying in the graveyard for many years before Revd John Snowdon had them erected on this site. They were moved into the base of the tower in 1983 to protect them from weathering and the effects of traffic fumes.

Interior of All Saints, 1904. Although of early foundation the present church owes much to Victorian reconstruction in 1860-61. The nave was lengthened by 16 feet, the chancel was rebuilt and the south porch was enlarged. This was achieved by moving the toothed archway stone by stone some 10 feet nearer to Church Street. The work took ten months to complete and cost £1,300. In 1880 a vestry was added and a new organ installed at a cost of £700.

Renovating the bells, 1939. In 1609 the church had one bell, a second was added in 1636 and a third in 1676. Excavations carried out in the tower foundations revealed the remains of a bell pit and furnace and it seems likely that these early bells were made on site by itinerant bell founders. In the early Victorian period there were still only three bells and two of them were cracked! The ringers were John (Donkey) Jackson, Thomas Stephenson and Phoebe Brown, who was appointed on the death of her husband. The three bells were recast in 1845 into six bells and two more were added in 1873. In 1891 the ringers were J. Mumford, W. Robinson, W. Beanlands, W. Cook, W. Waland, A. Critchley, Joe Beanlands and James Denby. In the following year plans were put forward to improve the bells as the peal was out of tune and damage was being caused to the tower, but it wasn't until 1939 that the bells were taken out and recast.

Wesleyan chapel, Wells Road, c. 1900. Following the move from the first chapel in Skipton Road, the new Wesleyan chapel was described 100 years ago as a 'handsome building in the early Gothic style, centrally situated in Wells Road, with a fine spire at the South West corner'. However, the church took quite some time to attain this handsome state. The foundation stone of the building was laid by Mr Edward Holden on 29 August 1868, and it had been intended that the church should be opened in 1869, but with building work behind schedule the ceremony had to be postponed until the following year. In the meantime, services were held in the schoolroom in the basement of the chapel. Even when the church was opened, the building still lacked a spire because of a shortage of funds, and this wasn't added until 1876. Likewise, money had to be raised for an organ and this was installed in 1872 at a cost of £480.

Interior Wesleyan chapel, c. 1960. The church is decorated for the Harvest Festival complete with a special loaf of bread on the organ! The numbers on the hymn board indicate that the service started with the well-loved hymn *Come, ye thankful people, come, raise the song of harvest home*. By the late 1960s the Wells Road church building had become an expensive liability and needed a great deal spending on it to correct the ravages of dry rot and other defects. A decision was made to demolish the building and move the church into the Assembly Hall. At the same time the Leeds Road Methodists suggested a union of the two societies and, in 1969, both congregations moved into a 'new' home in the Assembly Hall. The chapel was demolished in 1970 and Guardian Court built on the site.

Laying the foundation stones of the Wesleyan Assembly Hall, 10 July 1903. At the turn of the century, Revd Dr Thomas Bowman Stephenson, who was principal of the National Children's Home, returned to circuit work and came to Ilkley. Once here, he assisted in the establishment of the Wesleyan Deaconess College in Queens Road and then turned his attention to relieving the inadequate Sunday school facilities. The solution was the erection of the Assembly Hall opposite the church. One foundation stone was laid by Revd Bowman Stephenson, another by Mr S. Kellett and a third by Mrs Mary Hepton in memory of her daughters Emily and Polly.

Wesleyan Sunday schools, c. 1914. The Assembly Hall was opened in September 1904 and was used for Sunday schools and midweek activities. The Home Defence took over the Assembly Hall for the duration of the First World War. During the Second World War the West Riding County Council used the hall for educational purposes to cope with the influx of evacuees. The hall became the Ilkley Methodist church in 1969 and following union with the United Reformed Church was renamed 'Christchurch' in 1981. The members of the united church were faced with two buildings for one congregation. The decision was taken to restructure the interior of The Grove church and sell the Wells Road site. This was converted into flats (Chapel House).

Leeds Road Methodist church 1969. A group of Primitive Methodists began to meet in Ilkley in the 1850s. Their first meetings were in the room over the shop in Brook Street used earlier by the Wesleyans. Later, the Primitives moved to the vacated Wesleyan chapel and then to the Working Mens' Hall in Weston Road (later the Liberal Club and now the Playhouse). The site for a permanent church at the corner of Wharfe View Road and Leeds Road was obtained in the 1870s. The foundation stone was laid in May 1877, and in March 1878 the chapel was opened for public worship following a procession of over a 1,000 people from the fountain at the top of Brook Street down to the new building. A Sunday school was erected in 1916. The closing activities at the Leeds Road chapel took place in August 1969. The building was demolished in 1970 and is now a car park.

Leeds Road Methodist Concert Party, 1919. The Leeds Road chapel acquired a strong reputation for thespian and musical activities. This distinguished group comprises two boot and shoe repairers (cobblers); Robert Haxby whose shop was a wooden hut at the junction of Leeds Road and Bath Street (now the Model Shop), and Walter Firth who had a shop at the corner of Church Street and Hawksworth Street (now the Pet Shop). Included among the ladies are Winifred and Isobel Hodgson, and Florence Harland.

Interior, Grove Congregational church, *c.* 1970. A scheme for the building of a Congregational church in Ilkley began to take shape in the mid-1860s, and a plot of land on the corner of Green Lane (later The Grove) and 'the proposed new Riddings Road' was obtained in the Middleton land sale of 1867. The foundation stone was laid on Saturday 30 May 1868 by the Mayor of Bradford, James Law Esq. A bottle containing several documents and copies of the *Ilkley Gazette* and other newspapers was placed in a cavity in the stone. The church took thirteen months to build at a total cost of £6,119 7s 11d, of which two-thirds had been subscribed before the opening services. Gifts rapidly cleared the outstanding debt of £2,060. Among the benefactors were Sir Titus Salt (£400) and Sir Francis Crossley. Although much work needed to be done before the scheme was completed, the church was opened for services on 16 June 1869.

Improvements to the church were carried out in 1873 when a new pulpit and an organ were purchased for almost £900. In commemoration of his seventieth birthday on 26 March 1881, Mr T.P. Muff, of Muff & Co., Bradford presented the church with a clock for the spire. It cost £120. In 1910-11 a new organ was provided, the side galleries in the church were removed, the pulpit was moved from the centre to the side, and the caretaker's house enlarged. These alterations cost almost £4,000. Following the union with the Methodists, the church interior was totally reconstructed in 1984-85 at a cost of £250,000.

Leeds Road Congregational Hall, *c.* 1965. Towards the end of the nineteenth century there was a spate of house building in the Leeds Road area of the town. The Congregationalists resolved to erect a new mission hall in this area and in the meantime used a house, 24 Ashlands Road, as a temporary home for meetings and evening services. A plot of land at the corner of Dean Street and Leeds Road was purchased and on 30 October 1901 the foundation stone of the hall was laid, and by the following July the building was in use for worship. In 1905 four new classrooms were added at a cost of £413. In 1939 further extensions were carried out to the primary department. In June 1952 the hall celebrated its Golden Jubilee under the stewardship of Mr Arthur Crook. The hall closed in 1970. It was subsequently demolished to make way for a small block of flats.

St Margaret's church, *c.* 1905. Discussions to build a second Anglican church in Ilkley began in March 1873. By July plans had been prepared for a church to be called St Margaret's as a tribute to the daughter of the vicar at All Saints, Margaret Snowdon. The land was donated by Charles Marmaduke Middleton and the eminent architect Norman Shaw was invited to submit a design. His first design incorporated a substantial tower but when he visited the site he decided the building would be top heavy and could end up in the valley! In August 1874 a temporary church built by William Hartley was opened by the vicar designate, Revd William Danks. Foundation stones were laid on 1 May 1878, and the church was consecrated by the Bishop of Ripon, Dr Bickersteth, on 10 September 1879. The work and anxiety associated with the scheme had undermined the health of the Revd Danks who was reluctantly obliged to resign.

122

St Margaret's Centenary Procession, 16 September 1979. The procession, led by Revd Tom Levesley, Bishop Ross Hook of Bradford and the Honorary Assistant Curate of St Margaret's, Geoffrey Buckley, has congregated at the top of Brook Street to meet with a similar procession from All Saints church. In the background are the musicians of the West Yorkshire Metropolitan Police Band.

St John's church, Ben Rhydding, 1906. Anglican services at Ben Rhydding Hydro had been instituted by the vicar of All Saints, Revd Dr William Muntz, in the 1890s and by 1901 it was decided that a new church was needed. The former cricket ground at the corner of Bolling and Margerison Roads was purchased for £650 and in December 1904 a start was made on the nave and chancel. The church was consecrated on 16 December 1905 though building continued. In 1909 a parish room was erected and in July 1910 the west end of the nave and the newly completed tower were dedicated by the Bishop of Ripon, the Rt, Revd William Boyd Carpenter. The total cost over the six years of building was £10,000.

Ben Rhydding Church Hall, *c.* 1980. Methodist services in Ben Rhydding began in 1852 in the farmhouse kitchen of Wheatley Hall thanks to the hospitality of the farmer, Mr John Berry Mawson. As the fellowship grew over the next twenty-five years it was decided to build a Wesleyan church in the village and land was purchased at the corner of Wheatley Lane and Ben Rhydding Drive. When St Margaret's church was opened, their temporary building (the 'Tin Tabernacle') was sold to the Wesleyans and re-erected on part of the future church site in 1880. This supposedly temporary building remained in use for 100 years, serving as chapel, Sunday school, and church hall. It was finally demolished in 1981.

Foundation stone ceremony, Ben Rhydding Methodist church, 1908. In the 1890s, Revd John Wesley Silcox retired from the active ministry and took up residence at Wheatley Hall. Although retired he threw all his energies into fund-raising for the new church and by 1908 the required amount had been raised. Five foundation stones were laid at the ceremony in July by influential supporters and benefactors, including the now widowed Mrs Silcox. The costs of the building were: stone and masons work £1,577, joinery £813, plumbing £171, slating £94, painting £12 13s 8d, and interior oak fittings £505 – a grand total of £3,172 13s 8d.

Ben Rhydding Methodist church and Wheatley Lane, *c.* 1914. The church was opened on 10 June 1909. The shop at the corner belonged to Ellis Beanlands, the grocer. Before the building of the two rows of shops and houses at the start of Bolling Road, Ben Rhydding shops consisted of three small wooden huts that backed onto the orchard wall of Wheatley Hall. One was a butcher's shop, one a greengrocer's and the other was a newsagent and tobacconist. Indeed Bolling Road itself was only laid out in the 1890s. Prior to this the village was reached via Leeds Road and Wheatley Lane or by Ben Rhydding (also called East Moor) Road although this mainly served the hydro.

Golden Jubilee, Ben Rhydding Methodist church, 1959. Members of the church have assembled for a group photograph during the fiftieth anniversary celebrations on Saturday 13 June 1959. In the centre of the front row are the minister, Revd Elijah Green and Mrs Green. Other members of the organising committee were Mr and Mrs N. Tomblin, Mrs H. Waite, Mr and Mrs A. Robertson, Mrs L. Jennings, Miss E. Crabtree and Miss E. Vost, and Messrs A. Skinner, J. Spensley, H. Eagle, E. Harrison and F. Collier.

Children's Special Service Mission, the Tarn, *c*. 1910. The Children's Special Service Mission (the CSSM) was a Christian outreach movement supported by local churches. It was active in Ilkley during the summer months before the First World War. The CSSM still operates today at some of our seaside resorts. The postcard has been printed 'reversed' so that the wording on the flag can be read.

Sunday school get-together, in the 1940s. Children and teachers from the various Sunday schools in Ilkley attend an inter-denominational rally at the Wells Road Methodist church.

Interior, Myddelton Lodge chapel, *c.* 1925. The chapel, dedicated to the Blessed Virgin Mary, was built in 1825 by Peter Middleton (1786-1866) who also erected the Calvary (Stations of the Cross) in the grounds. Until the Church of the Sacred Heart was built in 1879, Roman Catholics in the area worshipped in this chapel. Those who had travelled a long distance were rewarded with dinner in the servants quarters after Mass. When the Passionist Fathers acquired the lodge in 1922, they renovated the chapel and it came into regular use after a lapse of thirty years. The chapel continues to be a place of worship for local Catholics.

The presbytery and Church of the Sacred Heart, Stockeld Road, *c.* 1905. The 'new' Roman Catholic church opened on 23 July 1879. The church was fitted with a pulpit and altar of carved oak transferred from the Myddelton Lodge chapel. Adjoining the church was a parish school built to accommodate 100 pupils. Miss Christina Carter was the headmistress in 1881. In 1969 the school moved to new premises in Valley Drive. In 1893 the presbytery was built on land next to the church, and the former presbytery at Myddelton Lodge was closed. Thanks to a legacy from James Clarke and his sister Sarah Foley (who had been pupils at the Sacred Heart School), the church was enlarged and completely refurbished between 1978 and '84.

Gathering at the Baptist church, in the 1950s. Revd G.H. Whittaker is surrounded by a large group of Sunday school children, Guides, Brownies, Boy Scouts, leaders and parents. The Baptist church held its first services in 1901 in a converted dormitory at Ilkley College. Soon afterwards the college was purchased by the Wesleyan Deaconess Order so new accommodation was required. The fellowship decided to press ahead with the first phase of an ambitious building project that included a main church with spire, assembly hall and schoolrooms. Building began in 1902 but, as it transpired only the hall and schoolrooms were completed, the former becoming the church.

Ilkley Cemetery, 1907. As a concluding photograph, the final resting place for many Ilkley residents might be considered appropriate. By the 1870s the graveyard at All Saints had become crowded and the Local Board were determined to provide a new cemetery. Two substantial fields between Leeds Road and the river, Great and Little Pybus, were purchased for £2,000 and, after approval by the Government Medical Inspector, building work commenced in 1876. Such was the pressure on space in the old graveyard that the first interment took place in the new cemetery in November 1877 before it had even been consecrated. Building work finished in 1878 and shortly thereafter the Bishop of Ripon carried out the consecration.